THE
MIDDLE
SEAT

THE

STOP CRAVING PLATFORMS

MIDDLE

START LOVING PEOPLE

SEAT

PEDRO LATORRE

"Sitting with Pedro over a cup of coffee is like drinking from a well of grace, compassion, and inspiration."

–Matt Lawson, Lead Pastor, Story City Church of Burbank, CA

"There are big differences between people who have to say something and people who have something to say. Pedro has something to say, and I hope you'll take the time to listen."

–Nate Ernsberger, Speakers Representative, Compassion International

"Pedro is the real deal. One of the best humans to walk this planet."

–Tyler Ward, Musician and YouTube Artist

"I wish that everyone in America had the privilege of being inspired first-hand by Pedro."

–Anjelah Johnson, Comedian and Actress

"I'm incredibly excited for you to read this book because the one thing I know you'll take from this is Pedro loves people."

–Manwell Reyes, Actor and Musician, Group 1 Crew

"Pedro is not only a gifted communicator and author, but he lives a life of love and compassion for people."

–Elijah Waters, Campus Pastor, City Church of Beverly Hills, CA

Special Thanks

Jessica LaTorre

Without you, life would be colorless. You have granted me grace, peace, and insight. I love you from the depths of my soul. I wouldn't be who I am if it were not for your words in some of my weakest moments.

My Family

All of you have been a part of the story that God has chosen to write thus far. Your words and actions have pushed me toward Jesus. Through all of the challenges, let's continue to choose love.

Erick Yamagata

Many of the following pages never would have been written without you.

Danny Canales

I am so thankful for your talent and your heart for the Kingdom.

Brent Ingram

Thank you for giving your time and creativity to this project.

City Church

Thank you to my pastors, leaders, and community for being generous with love.

CONTENTS

Foreword

Today I woke up with the intention of buying a plane ticket to fly home and surprise my wife who I have not seen in a month! Now I know what you're thinking . . . aw, he's so sweet! Yes, yes, I am. But what is irking me to no end is that the only seat left on the entire plane is a middle seat! I'm having nightmares of being squished between two football players whose shoulders are so wide they pour into my personal space the entire five-hour flight. Or that I sit next to Chatty Cathy and Snoring Marvin and have the option of talking about the newest items available on the Home Shopping Network or watching Marvin's lips quiver with every annoying sound that passes through them. Either way, it's going to be an uncomfortable ride unless I step back for a moment and view this thing in a different light.

What if Chatty Cathy needs me to listen to every word she has to say because she's never felt like anyone cared enough to be fully attentive to her passions? And what if Snoring Marvin snores because he's so tired busting his hump flying all over the country trying to provide for his wife and four beautiful kids? I no longer see a nightmare but God's dream for me to be love in a situation that may need it.

Pedro and I have had the privilege of touring the world together and have literally experienced the best and the worst of the middle-seat chronicles. Despite all that, I have seen his heart for people and his desire to see them come into a revelation of who God wants to be in their lives. We have shared stages and have rocked in front of thousands of people and at the same time encouraged one another backstage after the cheers have all faded away.

I am incredibly excited for you to read this book because the one thing I know you'll take from this is Pedro loves people. And let's be honest, we could all use a little more love in our lives. Enjoy!

–Manwell Reyes, CEO of Group 1 Crew

Introduction: Pre-Board

At this very moment, my life is pretty scary.

Maybe you can relate.

Even though it's a stormy season, I have a profound joy and an inner assurance—an inner confidence that somehow God is going to make sense of life's question marks. As I began writing this book, I quickly noticed that it was writing me. I thought I had something to say but actually found out I had something to see. While writing this book, I have found myself in a perpetual season of storms. My computer was stolen along with years of my sermons, writings, and ideas that I can never get back. My speaking career seems to be changing daily like the direction of the wind. One day I am speaking in a public school and the next I am in a random part of the country speaking at a church. I became a father and while it is amazing,

I am faced with many new challenges. My father was diagnosed with bone cancer and given a little over a year to live. While that in itself is difficult enough, I am also deeply grieved to be on the other side of the country from him. My father and I lost way too much time over the years because of the complicated dynamics of divorce. So in addition to being in an emotional whirlwind personally, this book has weathered its own set of attacks. My original publishing company, which was funding the launch of this book, completely dissolved its business. So now with deadlines quickly approaching we are about $1,500 short of being able to self-publish the book you are holding in your hands. Gosh. That's embarrassing but I need to be as real as possible right now.

The point is, life is not comfortable or easy in any way. I am not about to tie a pretty bow on this book and pretend it is all good. It's not. It has been through much angst and frustration that have since filled its pages. Maybe you are not necessarily in a storm but are looking for change or growth or what's next.

Maybe you're wanting to go deeper in your walk with God.

Maybe you're not sure what that looks like.

Maybe you're waiting to hear from God.

Maybe you're scared that God might try and change all the things you have come to love about yourself.

Maybe you're not sure that God even exists.

I have felt all these things at some point in my life. (Sometimes I feel all of them in the same day! That's real talk.)

It goes without saying—but usually after people say, "It goes without saying," they have something to say, which I do—we all have come in from different directions and situations. Some of us are coming off a long layover period in a relationship that was uncertain. Others have come in from a long peaceful drive through the mountains of success. No matter how you came to this book, I believe there is something for you in these pages. Something that will challenge you. Something that will encourage you. Something that will propel you to live and love differently.

We are told from the time we are children that we should chase dreams and do something incredible. I will go on record and say that dreams and ambitions are great things to possess. But why don't we spend an equal amount of time talking about people? After all, your wildest dreams can come true, but without people, you won't be completely fulfilled. Your bank account can be full and your heart can still feel empty. You can make it to the NBA, but if you don't have teammates to pass the ball to you won't go very far. I really believe that in all our pursuits and passions we have to see people the way God sees humanity.

What if we stopped craving platforms and got back to the reason Jesus stepped out of Heaven in the first place? For people.

What would our world look like if we were a place for real people, with real problems, to encounter a very real Jesus?

I want to propose that if anyone wants to change the world, it begins and ends with the middle seat. The middle seat is that seat at a doctor's office or on a plane that none of us wants but inevitably all end up in at some point. My intention is to question our perception of influence and challenge our goal-oriented way of loving people. I don't want to live my whole life seeing people as projects that need fixing or old homes that need renovating. I also don't want to view someone else's position as a means for me to become more successful. What a terrible way to live life. I believe we can live lives that are outside the cultural norms. I want to live a life that is marked by inclusive love, a genuine love that is without ulterior motive or selfish ambition. This way of living life begins when we see people the way God does. Life marked by sacrifice, love, and listening.

I am far from where I want to be on this journey in life, but I won't give up on the journey just because the first few steps were not comfortable. I hope that the same goes for you. Fasten your seat belt because this may get a little bumpy (pun fully intended).

CHAPTER 1: NOW BOARDING

It is 5 a.m. and tiny drops of water fall like shooting stars from your comfy window seat on Delta Flight 940. You are sending your last text message: "TEXT YOU WHEN I LAND." Now you post a tweet with a very predictable hashtag: "They say the early bird gets the worm, not true. #earlyflight." You power down your phone and double check that you actually fastened your seatbelt. You quickly drop your elbow on the armrest just so the person in the middle seat knows what time is—it's time to get some much needed rest. After all, you deserve it.

This book began with one thought I could not let go uncontested.

"I deserve the first-class upgrade. I've earned it."

Have you ever not gotten something you deserved? Have you ever auditioned for a part you were perfect for but didn't get it because someone else knew the director? Have you ever worked years for a promotion that the new guy received?

Well, if you haven't, don't hold your breath because you will be overlooked or underappreciated at some point. It's just life.

I hate the entitlement I see in my own heart. I really do. I hate it. It seems to be as faithful as the morning sun. It rises up every day, and I do my best to extinguish it before the sun goes down. Similar to the sun, I wonder sometimes, "Where does it come from?"

Why am I so focused on me? When did this gigantic planet ever sign up to revolve around me? John Calvin spoke to this unfortunate reality that exists in all of us. "Man's nature is a perpetual factory of idols," he said. Yep. That sums me up all right. My "wanter" never ceases to want. No matter how much I acquire, I am always left wanting a little more and a little more.

What John Calvin realized is that the underlying foundation on which all these idols is both erected and sustained is _____. Feel free to insert your name right in that blank.

Many of us have gotten caught up in the routine of life, and we are missing out on the joy of the exploration. I know that's true for me. I have a hard time existing in the only place I can exist.

Here. In this moment.

Even the most beautiful things can become monotonous if we don't choose to live in the moment. Our marriages can become monotonous. Our ability to smile or to carry on a conversation with a stranger can become monotonous. For these coming chapters, we will journey down the runway of life together and examine some crucial ideas and realities. I pray that you see the most common and mundane parts of your life as beautiful, powerful, and meaningful. I tell some stories that

I hope challenge you. I have some thoughts that I hope encourage you. I share some experiences that I hope make you laugh a little. But most of all I have a deep conviction that we need to be sharing our love in both word and action.

This is not about your performance. This is a book that was written to bring clarity and freedom to anyone willing to join the ride.

My hope is to provide you with a little bit of balance in a world of chaos and confusion. The takeoff may be accompanied by some turbulence but we are approaching smooth air shortly. Most likely!

It Started with Mary

Now I know what you're thinking, but I'm not talking about the mother of Jesus. But props to her because without her I wouldn't be writing this book! Anyway, I met a sweet old woman on a plane named Mary who launched everything you are holding in your hands. The concept behind my writing was not an idea but an experience. I was leaving a conference awhile back and was about to get on a red-eye flight from the northwest heading down to Florida. I was tired.

I remember having the exact thought, *Jesus, if you love me you will give me the window seat on this flight.* (Don't judge my conversations with Jesus, I tend to be pretty honest!)

So in light of that, allow me to be really honest with you. I was disgusted with that prayer the moment I prayed it. I knew even in that moment that my comfort was driving my desires rather than my willingness to be used by God. Nonetheless, I checked myself pretty quick and said, "Jesus, I'm sorry. Do whatever you want. Not that you need my permission."

Delta started boarding the flight, and as I stood up I could feel the exhaustion of traveling settling into my body. As I made my way onto the plane, I quickly observed that I had the middle seat. I remember cracking a smile and thinking, "You got me, Jesus!"

The middle-seat lifestyle is not about waiting for your emotions to align with your beliefs. It is about your beliefs reorienting your emotions. Don't get me wrong—your emotions will still be there on most days. Our goal in those moments is to do what we know is right even when we don't feel like it. Some would call this discipline, and it's something that I personally lack a lot of when it comes to loving people.

I climbed into my seat and quickly started turning off all my little devices so I wouldn't get distracted by anything. On my right sat an older gentlemen who made every effort to not look my direction. He was on a phone call, and it sounded pretty intense. So naturally, I turned to my left and an older woman sat down with a half smile on her face and said, "Good evening." I assumed that we would end up in a conversation of some sort, but I had no idea what it would do to me.

Her name was Mary and she came on the plane with a ton of baggage. I'm not talking about actual suitcases. Mary began unloading her whole life story on me before we were even in the air. I really had absolutely nothing to say, and that's exactly what she needed.

During the next six hours, we laughed together, cried together, and wrestled through some real life questions. Her son was in jail because of a meth addiction he had struggled with since middle school. Mary was now raising her son's daughter in his absence. She was on her own and feeling the pressures of being a parent when she should be enjoying retirement while spoiling her granddaughter.

Mary had been beaten up by religion, but she believed there was a God out there somewhere who maybe loved her. For six hours, Mary and I talked about almost every topic you can imagine. As she was clearing the tears from her eyes, she took a deep breath and exhaled a simple sentence that opened the door for me to share my story.

"So tell me about your life," she said.

I looked at her with a smile and said, "We are going to need another flight for that conversation!"

I began to share my story with Mary with as much honesty and truth as she granted me. It went something like this . . .

Turbulence

When I was seven years old, my mother and father gave up on their marriage and got a divorce. My father got down on his knee and pulled me close. "Son," he said, "you're the man of the house now. Take care of your mom, and take care of your sister."

My father didn't know it at the time, but those words wounded me so deeply. In that moment, I attempted to take on a burden and responsibility that should have never been mine to carry. My mom went on to marry one of my dad's best friends from high school.

Confusion. Fear. Displacement.

Those would be the words that would define much of my early childhood years. I went to more schools than I can even remember. I lived in more places before middle school than most people do in a lifetime. Movement became the comfortable norm. I traveled on planes like most people travel in cars (when your dad has visitation and you live a few states over, that tends to happen).

I watched my mom and stepdad fall in love. I saw what it meant to be broke and what it meant to be rich. I played baseball to escape every past hurt. It was my drug of choice. My stepdad and mom decided to give up on their marriage when I was in middle school, and yet again I had to say goodbye to another dad, as if once wasn't enough. I felt angry. I felt like I wasn't wanted at times. I struggled in school. I became a sought-after athlete. I was injured. I was told I would be great, and I was told I would never amount to anything. There were many times I would lie in bed at night and wonder what my purpose was on this planet. I often had way more questions than answers and way more fear than hope.

Mary interrupted me to ask me the question I had hoped she would ask: "How did you make it through all of that?"

My answer was quick and honest.

"Jesus."

I began to share with her that God had been my perfect father. That despite the imperfections and struggles of my earthly parents, my heavenly father was faithful and loving.

Over the next few moments, I was able to share the hope of salvation with Mary. I was able to tell her that God is a God who redeems. I let Mary know that God had restored and is continuing to restore my relationship with my family.

I told her that Jesus is bigger than every tear, fear, and doubt that lives in her. Soon, our time on that plane was coming to an end. I wanted so badly for Mary to accept Jesus right then and there. When something has changed your life like He has changed mine, all you want is for other people to experience it. I told her how to choose Jesus, how to repent and believe. I walked her through what that could look like right here on that plane. I told her that Jesus is offering her salvation for eternity and an unbelievable journey in this physical life.

She looked at me and said, "I believe there is a high power, but I am not sure it's Jesus." My heart sank into the bottom of that plane. It hurt to hear that response. I looked back at Mary and said, "Even if you don't believe in Jesus, He wants you to know that He believes in you. Mary, that could be why we sat next to each other tonight."

She had the most gentle smile on her face. I kept thinking she was going to say something else. We seemed to just linger in that moment for what felt like forever. I don't have some grand ending to this story that is going to give you chills and make you want to jump up and down. Here is the simple truth that changed my life that day. Jesus is not looking for people with answers. He is looking for people bold enough to ask questions and love Him and others in their doubt. Mary may never choose Jesus, but I know she knew that my middle-seat moment with her was beautiful. It was something heavenly. I did my best to plant a seed of hope in her soul. I pray God touches Mary's heart and woos her to Him.

For some of you, the story about Mary has a bad ending. You probably have a ton of questions and maybe even think I am a horrible evangelist. All I know is that Mary was not a project—she was a person, a real human with real questions far bigger than I will ever be able to answer. Some of you are taken aback by how bold I was in sharing my faith with Mary. Some of you probably wish I would have said more and handed her a

Bible. I did my best to share about the best thing that has ever happened to me. I did my best to be real with Mary.

God positions us in middle seats to be a doorway to Him, not a cheat sheet to all of life's darkest tests. I for one don't have answers for the pain of humanity. I just know who came and met me in my pain. I pray God opens our eyes to every middle-seat moment that's in our future. Let's not miss the potential of the now!

Why Would We?

Have you ever booked a middle seat on purpose? Of course you haven't. Not on purpose. Nobody in their right mind would select that seat. That's just dumb. It's not comfortable. I am one of those people who constantly asks, "Why do we do the things we do?" I know it is not the deepest question to ask but it is an honest one. I am just going to list out some reasons . . . . Better yet, I am going to list out all my own personal reasons. I can't write a book about honesty and not be honest. If you can't relate to any of this, then you either don't fly enough or you're just closer to Jesus. But either way don't judge me.

1. Some people aren't as skinny as others.

2. One person smells weird. Two people smell really weird.

3. Playing elbow war with an 80-year-old feels wrong (especially since I'm undefeated).

4. I don't want to feel trapped (sometimes duty calls, and I always report for duty).

5. I don't want two strangers trying to doze off on my shoulders (can you say *Tic-Tac*?).

6. I didn't spend all this money not to have a view (my Instagram is dying for the #sunsetpic).

7. I want to have a window to fall asleep on (and drool on and check out my reflection).

8. I want the aisle because then I don't have to scream for my peanuts.

9. I want the aisle so I can stretch out my legs a bit (and trip little kids).

10. Basically, I want comfort and so do you.

OK. Ten reasons should be enough for me to get this thing rolling. Do you notice what all those statements have in common? None of them display a genuine concern for anything other than me. It is so easy for me to make choices whether small or large with me and me alone in mind.

For some reason, my best attempts to be outwardly focused are often thwarted by some internal me-driven motor. The middle seat for most of us is where all the procrastinators sit. It's for Last-Minute Lucy going on vacation to Florida to see Mickey Mouse and get sun burned. It's for Late Nate going to New York because he loves big apples. Bad joke.

The bottom line is that the middle seat is not for the working class. It's for the talkers. The people who can have full-on conversations with 2-year-olds for hours. That's just not me, guys! I don't have time to waste on people. Are you kidding me? People are fickle. They are frustrating. They are . . . well, down-right annoying sometimes. Many of us would never say or even type those words, but if we are honest I think we all have days where those dark thoughts cross our minds.

Do you ever feel your switch turn off in a conversation because you realize this person has nothing to offer you? I have. Scary, huh? I tend to treat people or relationships like using my card at the ATM. "I don't want to have to put much thought into this, but I do want an awesome return." Is that how we were made to live? Are we missing something here? When did this identity theft happen? These are real questions that I have had to wrestle with in my lifetime. I want to be honest with you right now: This book isn't about a flight I took—it's about the way we have become accustomed to living.

This is not a book for those wanting me to demolish a way of living. I am not here on a soapbox reinforced with pride and perfection. I am coming to you from a place of true excitement. Yes, EXCITEMENT! I am excited to expose the lie about the middle seat. I am excited about even one person who sees truth in its purest form and embraces a new way of living.

You and I may have nothing in common, but we will never be sure until one of us risks the conversation. I am learning more and more every day that it is a risk worth taking.

Do Not Disturb

I was recently in the middle of a crazy month of traveling. I was playing drums on the weekends and then flying to conferences and speaking engagements on the other side of the country during the week. I got an email from the person who handled flights for the new band I had started drumming for, Group 1 Crew.

"What seat do you prefer when you are traveling on planes?" it said.

Without hesitation my fingers began to pound away with an almost knee-jerk response. "I don't care as long as it's not the middle seat."

I probably should have said what I was thinking: "Just keep me really far from human beings." On second thought, that probably would not have gone over well.

After sending the email, I quickly started reflecting. As I mentioned earlier, I have a tendency to do this. I began to analyze my words, and it got ugly fast. I don't avoid the middle seat just so I can rest. I don't avoid the middle seat just so I can go pee at the drop of a hat. I avoid *people*. I avoid connection. Interruption. Disruption. Noise. I put on headphones and listen to music or watch movies. I read books or prep for sermons I will be preaching. Come on. Seriously? Where did my love for people go? Have I ever had it? I mean, sometimes it's just bad. I probably shouldn't tell you this for fear that you might put this book down, but I have to be honest. Sometimes I even open my computer and leave it on just so people will assume I have work to do. It's like my 40,000-foot "Do Not Disturb" sign. If you're the person who really likes talking on planes and finding out where people are from and where they are headed, I think that's awesome . . . for you! It is just not my nature. I think part of it is that I was flying all the time and to be honest those superficial conversations drive me crazy. I like conversations with meaning and depth. I don't have time to talk about the Yankees bullpen. That is stuff for children! OK, not really; can you imagine two 4-year-old kids talking about the Yankees bullpen? Seriously, I might pause and listen to that. It would be so amazing!

I am pretty sure you think I am terrible person by now, so I need to pull you back in fast. I actually do love people. I promise I do. I was flying from Portland to Florida and I prayed some dangerous words. Before I tell you what *not* to pray, I will tell you what convicted me. That seems to be the more spiritual thing to do after unloading all my issues.

I was at an evangelistic conference learning things like how to choose your board members, how to develop a budget for your nonprofit, and how to plan and execute large-scale outreaches. I really was learning a lot and feeling encouraged. I was invited by a very cool California-based youth pastor and a Christian record-label owner to go check out a local donut spot that had a very anti-Christian name, Voodoo Donuts. I am pretty sure the donuts were not cursed with anything other than an insane amount of calories and the ability to leave your hands super sticky. As we climbed out of the car, a man briskly approached our vehicle. He seemed flustered and either ready to fight or ask some sort of important question. Either way, just for the record, I was totally ready to fight. No man stands in front of me and a perfectly unhealthy donut.

This man began to open up his heart, and right in the middle of downtown Portland, I experienced a powerful middle-seat moment. He began sharing his story with us. He told us his girlfriend had broken up with him, and he had come downtown to get some "booty." His words, not mine. He was lost and just needed some money to get home. Then that moment happened when we realized this guy was not asking for prayer. He genuinely needed money to get home. I saw the middle-seat opportunity right in front of me, and I wasn't going to miss it. I told the man I would give him some money for his trip home.

Now, hold up. I know you probably just got a little frustrated thinking that I supported this man's addictions and caused him to sink deeper into a pool of despair. But slow down, eager beaver! If you were thinking something along those lines, don't worry; you're human. Being that you're human, you know you have some addictions, as well. We all do. The bottom line is that I saw an opportunity. I saw an opportunity, and it came through his expressed tangible need to get home. Doesn't that sound familiar? God will use our hurts, habits, and hang-ups to draw us closer to Him. He is actually really good at it. What I realized in this exchange is that every single conversation you and I have with another human being is an opportunity to meet a need and satisfy a longing. And it is not always his or her need or longing that will be met. Sometimes it is yours. Sometimes it is mine. We will talk more about that later. Sorry for that tangent, but it felt necessary. OK, now back to the story.

We probably took about ten or minutes or so just standing on a street corner in downtown Portland talking to a perfect stranger in need of some cash. His name was Peter, and we gave that man money and Jesus. And Peter surrendered his heart to Jesus. He repented of his sin and proclaimed with tears in his eyes that Jesus was His Savior.

This story is not about the end result, though it was truly an amazing moment. This story is simply about seeing the opportunity and being willing to have an exchange. We could have just met his need and given him some cash and gone to get our sticky fingers on and felt like good, philanthropic humans. Honestly, we were not in some spiritually charged mood ready to evangelize in Portland. We just got done listening to a new hip-hop song and talking about what we thought about the lyrics. We were tired and craving some good junk food. If anything, we were probably a little over stuffed on Christian jargon and spiritual conversations. We just saw a need and met it. Need in its most basic form is an opportunity for humanity to engage with humanity. Need in its most spiritual form is an opportunity for humanity to tangibly experience the divine. When you meet someone's tangible need, your faith and belief in the Gospel becomes more evident to both you and him or her. It is from this place that we are called to love and serve people. I really believe we are just one conversation away from seeing God show up and show off all around us. It is not about your ability—it is truly about your availability.

Tuned In vs. Tuned Out

So many of us proselytize people and view them as projects. Come on, you do it, too. We all struggle to not judge the book by its cover. We look at what people wear and we deduce what they value. Now that we know their priorities aren't in order we deduce that they are lost and wandering souls who need to hear about Jesus. Every second we get, we try to shove a catchy saying down their throats or a tweet-worthy slogan. I am not trying to read your mail; if anything, I am reading you mine. So, what can we learn from all this, and why is it important?

We can't figure out what tangible needs people have if we aren't even willing to have a conversation with them. When we realize that we are all in need of human connection and relationship, we level life's playing field. It is from this place that we connect on a basic human level. Sadly, many of us see the word *conversation* and think that means "talk more." "Pedro, I am not good at preaching at people," you might be saying. Good. If people wanted a preacher, they would come to your church. The middle-seat life is more about listening. It is about being interested in others rather than trying to be perceived as interesting. It is about valuing others long before they give you a reason to.

The powerful thing is that when you are genuinely engaged and listening to other people, they grow comfortable with you. What if someone else choosing Jesus began with you physically positioning yourself in the center of his or her need? What if you are physically positioned right now where you are sitting for a reason? What if you took the headphones off long enough to enjoy a cup of coffee with a stranger and share some laughs? Who knows, you may be the one God will use to meet that person's need. Maybe he or she needs encouragement in that moment. Maybe he or she needs you to sympathize with him or her. Maybe this person just needs to vent and get some things off his or her chest.

Maybe the solution is not you proclaiming Jesus with your mouth but being Jesus with your life. It is a hard pill to swallow, but it brings so much life. Loving others like Jesus would in that very moment looks like being present in their problems, listening like Jesus would in that very moment, and being broken for others like Jesus was and is. It is about tangibly demonstrating the heart of the Savior and not just talking about Him as though He is not in the room.

He lives in us. He is ready even when you are caught off guard or feel unrehearsed. Demonstration is less about doing something and more about being something. Dare I say, it is being connected to something and ready to love well during life's layovers. Demonstration is dangerous—very dangerous— but so worth it!

Malibu and Money

Demonstration is a dangerous word to toss out to a bunch of us Christians. Honestly, even if you are not a believer at all it is still a really dangerous word. We quickly see that word and think bumper stickers and T-shirts. We are quick to make demonstrating God's love about weekend trips to clean up local highways or serve in the soup kitchen (all of which are awesome, so keep it up). Oftentimes we see demonstration as an event rather than a way of life. Don't get me wrong—I am all for mission trips, but if we are neglecting to notice our neighbor then we are missing what it means to follow Jesus. We cannot allow demonstrating the love of Christ to become a formula where if we say the right things and smile at the right moments, people will come to Christ. People are far more concerned with what our lives are saying when our mouths are shut than when they are open.

How you listen to people is a direct reflection of your knowledge of God's love for you as an individual and God's love for others. You can manufacture an interest in other people and take off your headphones and blah blah blah . . . but people can feel that junk. I can feel that junk when people do it to me. Have you ever been in a crowd of people trying talk with someone who is looking at everyone but you? Yeah, I have too! It's a horrible feeling. You wonder, *Why am I even trying to talk to you right now? You aren't even here in the moment.* You can force and fake demonstrative love for people, and that, my friend, is why it's dangerous. At some point, we have to choose to grow into an understanding or, dare I say, a constant realization of God's love for us.

That is where it all starts. Scripture uses the word *transformation*. As my pastor says, "We can't put a timeline on transformation." But we do need to be committed to the Transformer so we can experience full and rich lives. I never thought I would say *transformer* in this book. Boom. It happened! I feel good about it.

My wife and I live in Los Angeles, California. It has pretty much perfect weather all the time. Beautiful sunsets.

Very little rain. No humidity. Basically, an appetizer before the main course. Heaven! OK, that's a bit much, but this place is really awesome—so awesome that our families are always coming to "visit us." That just means that they want to go to beaches and cool restaurants. Good thing I really like both!

Awhile back my father, stepmom, and stepbrother came out to visit us for a week or so. We had a ton of fun until we decided to go to Malibu Cafe. I know it just sounds like dollars pouring out of your pocket, right? We got to this place and realized pretty quickly that the prices for the meals were well outside of our typical dining budget. I was committed to paying for this meal even if it meant I was going to have to take out a full loan. We bought their dinner, and everyone was just living it up. Except for me.

My wife told me we had to share a meal because of how expensive it was. Everyone else was ordering these elaborate dishes filled with awesome ingredients, and I was left there killing these appetizers. I did get some dessert though. As I was licking my lips trying to savor my last bite of chocolate cake, the waiter decided to come and bring me back to reality with the bill. I took a deep breath. He put the check on the table.

There was this really awkward pause on his part. He kept his hand on the check and finally looked up, slightly puzzled as were we, and said, "Garrett, the owner of the restaurant, has decided to pay your bill in full tonight."

"Um. What?" I said.

"Your bill has been paid in full," he continued.

My family and a couple of our friends who joined us for dinner (probably because they knew I would pay) began to celebrate like their team just won the Super Bowl. I was not happy. I was not OK with this. Had I known that someone was going to pay for the meal, I would not have split a meal with my wife. I was driving home thinking, *Can we do that all over again? Can I get one more chance to order everything on the menu?*

My point in telling you this story is very simple. I believe all our lives are like my experience that night. Do you know how many people I have told about that restaurant? That owner had no reason to bless us. We had nothing to offer him, nothing but gratitude. I really do believe this is what the Christian life is all about. It is about obsessing over God's love for us. It is about living in a constant awareness of God's goodness, love, and favor, which is aimed right at us.

That is how we become effective. That is how God's love is going to advance to all corners of the Earth—when we wake up each day with a deep awareness of God's love. I am all for theology, but if we lack an awareness of God's intimate love, then we are missing the flight. We are missing out on full lives.

In the book of 2 Corinthians 13:5, Paul gives us a spiritual litmus test. He basically says, "Test yourself in this, and see if you are a maturing believer. Do you have a growing awareness of God's activity and movement in your life?" It's that simple. If we have a growing awareness of God's activity in and through us, we will venture into the unknown because we have a peace that passes all understanding. That peace is a person, and He has a name. That peace is Jesus, and He will cause us to live lives that are built on the strongest foundation known to man. Love. God-designed and God-given love.

The Point of No Return

When pilots of old were flying planes for exploratory missions, they often came across a dreaded moment. They called this moment "the point of no return." This was when they had enough fuel to either play it safe and turn around or stay the course and venture into the unknown, not knowing if or where they would land. I believe all of us need to have a strong understanding of God's deep love for His people and be willing to venture into unknown conversations. Out of that awareness, our ability to demonstrate the passionate love of God will become refreshing for the spiritually thirsty. So will you consider putting this read down just for a moment to spend some time observing God's love for you through His Word? Hopefully you are cool with that. Open your Bible to John 9:1–7. Read it. Read it slowly. Read it twice. Ask God to speak to you through every detail that is given to you and even the details that He chose not to give to you. It was all written for you and me to grow in our awareness of the God-Man, Jesus. When you come back, we will examine these scriptures together. We will choose to move forward in the journey. We will choose to love when it hurts and is inconvenient. Go and breathe deeply of Him.

Jesus Postpones His Flight

There are so many beautiful parts to this story. If you are anything like me, there is a 50/50 chance you did not pause and read the passage because you are tired or your phone is dying. I get it. No shame in that game. Here are some initial things that have recently stood out to me about the story of the blind man and Jesus found in John 9:1–7:

Verse 1: "As he passed by, he saw a man blind from birth." Jesus was walking. He wasn't running a campaign or promoting himself.

Verse 2: "And his disciples asked him, 'Rabbi who sinned, this man or his parents, that he was born blind?'" Notice the followers of Jesus trying to find the cause of the man's issue rather than the cure.

Verse 3: "Jesus answered, 'It was not that this man sinned, or his parents, but that the works of God might be displayed in him.' Jesus speaks to the purpose of this man's condition.

Verse 6: "Having said these things, he spit on the ground and made mud with the saliva. Then he anointed the man's eyes with the mud . . . ." If God can use spit and mud, He can use us!

Verse 7: ". . . And said to him, "Go wash in the pool of Siloam," [which means Sent]. He went and washed and came back seeing.

Jesus showed himself to be concerned with the man's problem, and His concern led to action. Compassion without action is just observation. Let's be real—He could have said, "Listen, man, I have a world to save, and this really doesn't line up with my supreme schedule today."

In the scope of the Jesus narrative, we find these seemingly small moments to be the most revealing of His character and deep love for humanity. Could it be that our demonstration in every seemingly insignificant moment is actually a billboard of God's deep love for humanity?

The funny thing about this story is that no matter how many times I read it, I never see myself as the blind man. It's easy for me to read a story like this and even point fingers at the disciples' accusatory slurs about this man's state.

But if we're honest, I think we all have found ourselves pointing more fingers than any of us would like to admit. This story embodies the nature of our King Jesus. He was going about His day and found himself in the middle seat between the disciples and a blind man. I am sure He could have had a billion reasons to keep on pace and focus on other "bigger" tasks. However, it appears that Jesus was not checking off a to-do list or was too busy to postpone a flight so that someone else could experience the goodness of His love.

I have found that the areas of my life that feel most rushed are the areas where I am ignoring people in my life who need my attention. Some of us are living run-on-sentence lives, jumping from one thing to another like a kid at Chucky Cheese. Some of us need to allow more space for commas and moments for pausing.

Our generation is sometimes too concerned with hobbies to focus on the wholeness the Gospel longs for us to enjoy. Oftentimes we equate business with effectiveness. The problem with this is we can start believing that an effective life is a busy life. Let's look at this on a little more practical level. I love to work out and go on hikes with the best of them. But the Lord has had me pause and ask Him to show me what the best use of my time is each day. Sometimes I find myself doing the same activities I wanted to do but with a friend who needs my attention. Other times, I find my schedule and my wants getting switched up, but always for the better. Our desires for our days don't even come close to His desires for our days. Don't let good things become your god and distract you from His will. Jesus was the best at this because He didn't let the mission interfere with the moment. Moments are what Jesus built His movement on. Let's take time to ask Jesus to show us the areas in our lives that are hurried, worried, or overstuffed. Allow Him to throw some mud on your spiritual eyes so you can see like He sees and value people over anything else. It's not about platforms friends; it's about people.

I pray you choose the middle seat in every area of your life and overflow in every conversation with genuine love. This isn't an act of will but an act of willingness. It begins with a daily walk with Jesus.

The sixteenth president of the United States, Abraham Lincoln, said this in regard to problem solving: "Give me six hours to chop down a tree, and I will spend the first four sharpening the axe."

I think this is a beautiful example of the value of prayer. Prayer sharpens our tongues to speak like Jesus. Prayer prepares our hearts to respond like Jesus. Prayer clears our ears to hear the very voice of Jesus. It will often feel like wisdom to start chopping your tree down with aggression and power. But the reality is that prayer will make chopping the tree down far more effective. Prayer makes sharing our faith far more effective. We learn to listen more and talk less. Prayer teaches us to speak with conviction that is lathered in love. Do not believe the lie that I have believed for many years, the one that says, "Get to work chopping down the tree." If our work precedes our worship, we are in trouble. We work and share our faith as believers as an overflow of our worship. Prayer aligns us with the reality of Heaven and equips us to do the work of Jesus.

The Word and presence of God must motivate everything we do. I think sometimes we can all complicate this heavenly reality with which God wants us to live. The truth is, if we want to look and act like someone or something we have to spend some time obsessing over the why and not the what. Why do we live on planet Earth? Why do we need Jesus? These questions will define what we do and how we do it. Let's spend our lives asking questions that matter to a God who cares. What we obsess over is ultimately what we will become. I encourage you to take inventory on that last statement before you start the next chapter.

CHAPTER 2: ECONOMY OF COMFORT

I hate waiting. Seriously. If you want me to have a terrible day, just make me stand in line. My friends don't even invite me to theme parks anymore because they already know what the answer will be. Also, a small but very important contributing factor is that I really hate germs. Being someone that travels a lot has helped me overcome, or at least cope with, lines and germs. There is nothing worse to me than flying for several hours on a plane only to land and spend another half hour waiting on a gate to become available. I feel like every sneeze and cough is going straight into my lungs, probably because it is. Has this ever happened to you? It's annoying, right?

When it comes to following Jesus, you will find yourself waiting a lot. At times you may even trick yourself into believing you are waiting on the Lord, as if He is late to your party. But waiting on the Lord doesn't mean He is late—it just means we need to slow down and posture our hearts for listening. The David we read about in the Bible is such an incredible example of waiting throughout his whole life. It seemed that David was always waiting on something or someone else. There was a long season of his life where he knew he would become the next king but still had to wait. Not only did he have to wait, but while he was waiting, he was also running for his very life. Doesn't that sound familiar? It does to me. It's often when I am waiting on God to give me clarity that I feel like life is going at 200 mph. Some days I am even tempted to just do it my way and hope it works out. I will go on record, though, and say it rarely works out well for me when I jump the gun.

As we zoom into the Psalms, which were primarily written in caves as David was running from King Saul, we can draw a couple of conclusions. These conclusions are by no means exhaustive, but some details have caught my eyes over the last couple years. One thing that pops off the pages in the Psalms is that David is constantly saying, "My soul waits on the Lord." We really can't understand the depth of what is being said here without defining the word *soul*. For me, I hear the word soul and immediately think of Casper the Friendly Ghost. If you weren't born in the '80s, you may not remember Casper. All you need to know is that he was very friendly! Our soul can be defined as the sum of our mind, will, and emotions. So David was showing us what it means to wait on the Lord. We choose to submit our minds to Him daily because we know that His thoughts are higher than ours. We choose to submit our will daily because we know that He has a plan far superior and more satisfying than ours. Last, we choose to lay down our emotions because His Spirit in us becomes our greatest point of focus. David was not saying that our souls do not matter to God. It's actually quite the opposite. David is trying tell us that everything we are should wait for everything He is because He is fundamentally greater. Waiting on God helps us remember who is ultimately in control: God.

Here is just one small example of David feeling his own emotions pushing in on him and choosing to redirect his focus. "Why am I discouraged? Why is my heart so sad? I will put my hope in God! I will praise him again—my savior and my God!" (Psalm 43:5, New Living Translation).

The truth about life is that we will have some emotionally exhausting days. I like that phrase at the beginning of the verse, "I will put." It shows us that this is an active choice on our part. Everyone around us is choosing to put his or her emotions into something. David is helping us see that when God is our source, everything will shift. It also caught my attention that he said, "I will praise him again," which implies that at some point he stopped praising him. Gosh, this is exactly what happens to me in my own life. When I begin shifting my eyes off Jesus, I inevitably begin worshipping or focusing on my emotions and false realities. Life gets really heavy and borderline impossible when I am in this kind of place. What you and I praise and hold in high esteem is what we treasure.

So what are you holding in high esteem as you read this book? This is a question I have to ask myself constantly. It's like a tune up for my soul every time I ask it, and more important, every time I honestly answer it.

If you are restless and discouraged, I want to strongly urge you toward examining your ultimate source for hope. Many Christians live out their faith in a way that is similar to an airport. I thought about this recently while I was picking up someone from the airport. The airport serves as a close replica to the Christian heart. On the outside, Christians have a genuine love for people. But on the inside there is nothing but chaos, confusion, and TSA lines. (OK, maybe not the TSA lines, but you can't write a book that is centered around the airport and not mention how terrible TSA lines can be! I have missed more flights than I would like to admit because of the TSA.) For many believers, our faith is robotic and mechanical.

We are missing out on the intimacy of exploration and the deep joy of adventure. I am persuaded to think that we are missing it. Jesus doesn't want us to go through the motions and hope we don't mess up too much. He doesn't want us living confused and chaotic lives not knowing how to wait on Him and enjoy Him. So many young millennials have given up on Jesus because they have seen too many curbside Christians. Curbside Christians are nice when everything is nice. People need to see Christians who are anchored to truth. When we are anchored to God's truth we will find intimacy with God instead of enmity with God.

Most of my walk with the Lord has felt like sitting in traffic. Not only do I not want to be sitting in the traffic, but I sit so long that I also forget where I am even going in the first place. I have spent so many seasons grumbling and frustrated that I am not where I want to be in this journey. I think if you are honest you maybe can relate to those feelings, as well. I recently was spending some time with the Lord and I heard Him speak to my heart so clearly.

He said, "Your greatest weapon, is waiting."

Could it be that our strength is truly renewed as we wait on the Lord? Could it be that our perspective on who is truly in control is forged as we wait on Him?

I believe David was running for his life in more ways than one. He certainly was running for his physical life, but he was also running toward his spiritual life. Those caves shaped David's awareness of God's voice and his belief in God's Word. Many scholars believe that he would actually scream out some of the scriptures he was writing and the cave walls would bounce his voice back to him. He utilized the waiting in the caves to strengthen his inner man. He practiced ingesting the Scriptures while he waited on God. When was the last time you spent time in the Word and allowed your soul some moments to marinate on its realities?

I truly believe our greatest weapon is waiting. As you wait in your cave of suffering or uncertainty, begin considering the potential of what God is shaping in you. You may feel like you are running from something, but you may actually be running toward something. Don't let the holding pattern you are in keep you from growing. Don't let the holding pattern keep you from knowing God on a level that you otherwise may have never thought possible. The cave is preparing you for what God has prepared for you. David needed the caves so that he could become the king he was destined to be. You and I need the caves to become the men and women God has called us to be. Your caves will shape your convictions, and your convictions will begin shaping your desires. This means that suffering and fear no longer can rule your life!

Free Falling

Sometimes I think people are downright crazy. Have you noticed how many people line up to willingly free fall at theme parks? They are paying for a piece of machinery built by humans to drop them out of the sky or propel them forward at insane speeds. People are paying people to make them feel afraid. I still cannot wrap my head around why people do this, but I was having a conversation the other day that gave me some insight. I was hanging out with my brother-in-law Josh and he said, "You know, we are born with only one fear—the fear of falling." He wasn't talking about the fear of falling in love, although I know a couple of people who seem to have that fear. He was talking about the feeling of actually falling over or falling from something. You ever see someone act like they are dropping their newborn baby? If you have and did nothing about it, what does that say about you? (Just kidding, lighten up!) My observation has been that the baby will instantly start crying and then eighteen years later it will run to the most expensive college it can find just for payback! Think about that the next time you throw your kid toward the ceiling fan! I know I will.

I totally think this fear-of-falling thing is true. Have you ever been deep in sleep on a flight and hit some turbulence? Or have you ever seen other people's reactions when they wake up to the jolting force of strong winds or an air pocket? It's actually pretty amusing. One time my wife and I were flying to visit some family, and we were on a smaller plane than usual.

She was feeling a bit apprehensive about getting on this paper airplane of a contraption. I would like to consider myself a traveling veteran so I, of course, comforted her, saying it was normal and everything was going to be fine. I think I even told her that smaller planes make for smoother flights . . . which is not at all true.

Well, about thirty minutes into the flight the pilot gets on his little walkie-talkie thingy and very nervously begins to explain that we are flying right into a storm and there is no way around it. Anytime a pilot starts talking in a whispering breathy voice you should be nervous. He doesn't actually want you to know that he is scared or that you are not safe. My hands instantly started sweating. All of my wife's irrational fears now suddenly had validity.

I started to feel exactly what she was feeling but couldn't let her know that because I am a man, and men don't act scared on planes. That's the stuff of babies. We started hitting some serious turbulence on the flight, and my insides were doing karate. It was like Jackie Chan was filming an instructional video in my stomach. It was terrible.

The lights on the plane started to flicker. *What in the world is going on right now? Should I have brought my night light? A Snuggie maybe?* Come on, you know you have one, too! I was gripping the seats like my life depended on it because I am pretty sure it did.

Jessie looked at me in this moment, needing me to be a real man, needing me to be strong. With tears in her eyes, she said, "Baby, is everything going to be OK?"

I was like, "Girl, we about to die." I am a really honest guy in high-stress situations.

Obviously, we made it off the plane in one piece, but my fear of falling was amplified that day. Free falling hundreds of feet at a time is not what I imagined when booking that flight.

I think we all have a fear of falling in life. Think about all the decisions you made today up until this very moment. Every one of them was calculated even if it was the smallest choice you made. You chose to use toothpaste to brush your teeth and not conditioner. You chose to use deodorant instead of laundry detergent under your arms. (Good choice, by the way, I feel like I should pause and congratulate you on that one.) The point is, we want to calculate and rehearse and plan and predict, don't we? Something in us craves security. Stability. Safety. No falling. No paper-airplane rides through storms.

We want the formula for everything, and to be honest, friends, it's safe when we live like that. We don't have to be afraid of flying if we are the pilot, right? We don't have to worry about the storms, if we are in the cockpit, right? So not true. If you have lived for any length of time, you have learned that most if not all of life is out of your control. No matter how much you plan your day or your moments, you can't plan for storms. You can't create margin for calamity or grief. What are we going to do when cancer comes knocking? What are we to do when we don't pass that test? Where do we turn when our dreams get pulled out to sea by our own fears and anxieties?

You and I cannot control anything. No matter how hard you try, you can't will your heart into beating. You and I don't own or control anything on this side of Heaven. So if we shift our attention off life's limitations, fears, and uncertainties, is it possible that we might discover a new way of living? We might even discover the way we were created to live.

I believe life is for everyone but truly living is for few. How do we come alive in light of our fears and differences? How do we breathe without worry when we can't control our own breath? I think the secret to the answer is found in one simple reality. When we are anchored to the truth of God's divinity and love for humanity, we find a life worth living. We find a hope worth talking about. We begin to thrive in moments of doubt because we are connected to a reassuring answer: The person of Jesus.

I believe that life's biggest interruptions are some of God's biggest invitations. Could it be, friends, that this massive God wants to invade your moments of frustration? What if all of life's detours were just destiny in disguise? Most, if not all, of the stories I share with people across the country were moments defined by opposition and tension.

I am confident that opposition is a breeding ground for opportunity. I have found that some of my most profound moments or seasons of growth have been when I was under intense pressure. Pressure provides us with perspective.

Many times when I feel pressure, I resort to performing. If my wife and I don't have enough money to pay our bills, I pick up more gigs and start selling more on eBay. I love selling and buying stuff on eBay! It's when I run out of gigs and shoes to sell that God usually gets my attention. "Pedro, this was never your story to write," I hear Him say.

We serve a God who longs to join us on this scary plane ride we call life. In the storms and in the chaos, He longs for us to find rest and peace, mainly because when you roll with Jesus, you have access to rest and peace because that is the very nature of Him.

Do you remember the story of Jesus and the disciples in the boat during the storm? The storm was real, friends. The waves flooding the boat were real waves. They were cold waves that tasted salty and burned their eyeballs. Let's not be so quick to view these guys as melodramatic and a waste of God's rescuing power on planet Earth. These men were human beings, and they were *being* smart by *being* scared, if you ask me. Jesus is not trying to override your senses; He is trying to turn your heart's attention to Him and grant you a restful and peaceful soul in the midst of life's free fall, a soul that over time may go from scared to walking on water.

So does this mean we need to run out and get ourselves into a heap of trouble and distress? No, of course not. Life will throw you enough curveballs—you don't need to go looking for them.

God will use our aspirations and desires to propel us toward Him. God is really good at taking everyday moments we surrender to Him and making them amazing. I just spent the last two hours at a coffee shop in an unexpected meeting. The meeting was supposed to be about my good friend Erick's interest in working with our nonprofit organization, but instead it turned into one big cosmic setup by God for both of us. I asked Erick how things had been going with his family back in

Las Vegas, and he immediately got real honest. I love honesty. It's so powerful!

He talked about his concern for his family and their financial state. As he spoke, I could hear that this was really a bigger problem than money. Erick went on to tell me that he just wanted his parents to have peace beyond their situation. His family had allowed some tough times to affect how they loved and spoke to each other. I think we all struggle with that from time to time. But what amazed me most about the conversation is what Erick said at the very end just before we parted ways. It was almost as though God set up this moment just for me to hear one simple message.

Erick said, "When people show me their worst, I want to give them my best." Wow! Isn't that the nature of Jesus? Isn't that what He has done for lost and broken people like you and me? We see this very same spirit in the book of Ephesians where Paul pens these beautiful words under the influence of the Holy Spirit.

But God, being rich in mercy, because of the great love with which he loved us, even when we were dead in our trespasses, made us alive together with Christ—by grace you have been saved—and raised us up with him and seated us with him in the heavenly place in Christ Jesus, so that in the coming ages he might show the immeasurable riches of his grace in kindness toward us in Christ Jesus. -Ephesians 2:4–7, English Standard Version

Come on! Those words *even when* just jump off the page and slap me every time (in a good way!). God is an *even when* God. He loves us even when we are running away. He cares for us even when our hearts are hard. If He loved us even when we were dead, then He surely loves us right now in this moment. God has given us His best in Jesus and so we now have the ability to give our best to His people. That's where it all starts, friends. Recognizing what God has done for you is the best thing you can do for Him.

Erick reminded me of why God's love is so powerful. It allows us to live a life beyond ourselves. I want that kind of life. I want to live an outward-focused life, constantly looking for opportunities to love people the way God has loved me. I want to live generously with my money even when I don't have as much as I would like in the bank. I want to live generously with my home even when I am tired of doing so many dishes from having people over all the time. Jesus has been far too open handed for me to live close fisted.

Are there people in your world who need that kind of love? I know there are plenty in mine. What if whole cities started loving people with this kind of selfless love that can only come from a selfless God? What would our world be like? I think it may feel a little more like hope and Heaven than any of us could ever imagine possible.

What is stopping us? What is stopping you? I think we could all answer these questions with a host of different responses. But there is one thing I think we are all struggling with and we have to address it.

Success. Yeah, weird, I know. More specifically, *perceived* success.

Perception Is not Reality

We live in an age where perceived success is more important than success itself. In other words, we want people to think we are successful far more than we actually desire to be successful.

This is super common out where I live in Los Angeles. We have people buying $35 salads with quinoa while they are out in public but eating peanut butter and jelly for every other meal at home. We have people driving $70,000 cars but sleeping in bunk beds in a place with ten roommates. I'm not knocking it—if your driving experience is that important to you, then do your thing.

But the reality is we all spend a lot of time, money, and resources trying to falsely advertise ourselves. At the end of the day, we are all trying to add value to our lives. Many voices in our culture would say we have the power to add value to our lives. But that can't be true. If this was true then clothes, cars, and careers would give us more than momentary satisfaction. If it were our responsibilities to add value to our own lives, we would pop out of the womb with the Apple Watch on, ready to schedule some meetings and ask Siri for directions to the nearest Starbucks.

Anything that was not with us at the moment of birth is an addition. An add on. Extra. More. I am not proposing that this stuff is bad. All things can be enjoyed appropriately and stewarded with God's help. I am merely suggesting that we may have an innate desire to cover up an innate need. In other words, the way we satisfy our sinful nature is masking our deepest God desires.

The Bible calls it sin. We chase cravings. We chase stuff. We chase opportunity. We chase success. We chase views on our YouTube channels, but what we are searching for is value. Meaning. Why am I here? Why did God breathe His breath into my lungs? Is there a purpose for me on this planet other than to suck oxygen and wear designer jeans?

This isn't just a "worldly" idea either. This sickness has captured the hearts of believers for centuries. Go back to the days of the OGs (*original gangsters*) of the faith. Think back to the Pharisees who were obsessed with the Law and not just keeping it but adding to it, as well.

The problem with success is that if you and I are the ones defining it, we will always build what feels good and looks good but won't stand the test of time. I mean, look at our Instagrams, for crying out loud! We are obsessed with posting pictures that make life look like a literal walk in the park. "Oh, this picture on top of the Alps? No bigs. Just a weekend trip with the homies. Trying to step up my cardio for my thirty-day on-foot journey around the Earth." What? You probably got those pictures off Google Images!

We love making people love us. We may not get their friendship, but we will settle for their envy. What is that? Why are we so yucky? If the world was blind, how many people would you and I really impress? Better yet, would impressing people be our aim at all?

The Gospel calls us to live a full life on the inside—to go on a journey with the Creator of all things and allow Him to be in all of our seemingly insignificant in-between moments. Some of us will do anything to be perceived as a put-together and a healthy member of society. You are a good family man. You love your kids and take your wife out to dinner every now and then. But what about your soul, friend?

Jesus didn't come for healthy, put-together people. He came for broken people. Scared and scarred people. The sooner you and I remove our needs for perceived comfort, we will find a true place of belonging.

We can come to Jesus with our filters and frailties. We can. The beauty in Jesus is that as He peels back the fake, we get to discover a real freedom. As He restores us back to our original design we find colors so beautiful and vibrant we will wonder how we ever lived any other way.

I believe Jesus is calling us to live a life of faith while fear is pressing in and making its presence felt. What if we could live a comfortable and confident life in the midst of great opposition? What if that is actually how we were made to live?

I do think we are afraid to fall, but isn't that what makes life awesome? I have hundreds of stories I could have started this chapter off with, but I chose the one of me acting like a child on that plane. I chose the one that was so insanely scary and frankly terrifying. Why? Because in my discomfort I had to anchor myself to something bigger. I had to be reminded that I am not in control, that I am not a veteran of all things life. I have fears and they are as real as my fingers typing on this keyboard. They scream loud in moments of silence. Fear is powerful when we give it to God. Fear can reinforce our humanity and shift us closer toward His divinity. His goodness. His love. His care for ordinary people, like you and me.

God wants us to find rest in this life, not just in the life to come. If you are a believer reading this, I want you to know that you are housing the answer. Quite literally, God's presence is present in you. Rest is yours. Rest is residing inside of you.

Have you ever heard someone say, "Perception is reality?" No, it's not! That's such a cop out. Perception is . . . well, our *perception* of reality. How I perceive reality does not change the reality. How I perceive truth does not change truth. Have you ever gone to see a 3-D movie? If you have, you probably had to take out a small loan because it's ridiculously expensive, right? After selling all your earthly possessions and then buying a ticket to the movie, you are handed a pair of horrifically ugly glasses. Not only do they want all your money, but they want your self-confidence, too! You sit down and quickly forget about the money you spent because the chair feels like God himself made it. I guess it kind of was—I crack myself up! That's pretty funny, guys, smile! The movie starts, and you put on the dumb glasses because if you don't you can't actually see anything. The screen is just one big fuzzy mess. That's what we all have to look forward to in old age. The glass is half empty, guys, but somebody has to be realistic. The point is that the glasses didn't change reality, it only changed our perception of reality. The movie from its infancy was formatted for a 3-dimensional experience. The glasses don't change the truth; they just allow us to see the fullness of what has always been.

God wants us to see the fullness of all He has always been. I will even go a step further and say that God wants others to see in us the fullness of all He has always been. He has always been faithful. God wants to display His faithfulness in and through you. God has always been loving. He wants to display His deep love and concern through you. Now your life is no longer craving additives or extras because you are living full of Him. You don't need any drug to give you peace when you have experienced this kind of hope.

In the book of Romans, Paul articulates the heart and desire of Jesus for the believer. Notice the words he used. Read this slowly: "May the God of hope fill you with all joy and peace in believing, so that by the power of the Holy Spirit you may abound in hope" (Romans 15:13, English Standard Version).

Fill. All. Power. Holy Spirit. Abound. Hope. These words are so powerful. So rich.

Do you want a full life?

A powerful life?

A life led by the very presence of Jesus?

A life that matters and counts?

A life that is a well of hope from which others may drink?

How do we get it?

Do we read more?

Do we pine for more success and a bigger platform?

Do we climb the proverbial success ladder of life and hope we arrive somewhere that isn't too shabby in the end?

No. We let go of every false God that is constantly trying to take the number one spot on the thrones of our hearts. We let the person of Jesus invade our existence. Jesus doesn't ever waste His presence, and if you're a believer, He has chosen to house it inside of you.

So, if you and I will allow Him to supply meaning and value, then that means all of life now has meaning and value. Every moment matters. Every human matters. Every moment has potential. Not because of your gifts. Not because of your resources. Not because of your platform, but because Jesus will multiply all that you surrender. Let's together be a people committed to giving Jesus with all that we are. That kind of life starts with letting Him into the confines of your soul.

Every day.

Every moment.

Right now.

CHAPTER 3: CHECK YOUR BAGGAGE

Baggage sucks! There is really just no other way to say it. I will never understand why some people even step foot on planes. Have you ever noticed that it is the people who don't need to check their bags that do, and the people who do need to who always want to carry it on?

Hey, guy who went on a weekend trip to Aspen with one jacket, some shoes, and a souvenir for your kid, bring your bag on the plane, bro. Why are your checking your bag? You could barely fit a rabbit in that suitcase. Hopefully, you did not put a rabbit in your suitcase. Hey, other dude who just came back from traveling the world ten times over, check your bags, bro!

Have you seen this guy before? Everyone on the plane gives him the stare. It's his fault, though. He gets on the plane in a full sweat like he just got mono or something! Seriously, I would be sweating that bad, too, if I just pulled a baby zebra twenty terminals.

This is out of hand. This is the guy who spends nothing short of five minutes trying to figure out how he is going to get his baby zebra into the overhead compartment. Then the flight attendant usually comes and with a voice of frustration says, "Sir, wheels out." What she is really saying is, "Sir, please use common sense." Then the guy clearly sees that the suitcase won't fit in the overhead compartment, but then will start looking around as though the plane has different-sized overheard compartments. *Bro, this is not a puzzle, it's a plane. They are ALL THE SAME SIZE.* The all caps right there was not me being angry. Seriously, it wasn't. It was the zebra's hoof hitting my elbow as this guy just went by!

The truth is, we all have some baggage. Some of us live in denial of it, but we all have it. How are we supposed to love other people when we feel so unlovable? How are we supposed to personify Jesus when we feel so heavy and empty all at the same time?

I think this is probably one of the most beautiful parts about Jesus. He will use who we are to minister to people right where we are. There are people probably sitting near you right now who are wrestling with their belief in God or even God's belief in them.

They don't need some future you.

They don't need some perfect you.

They need the God you lean on like a bike needs a kickstand.

They need to see your dependence.

They need to see your reliance on Jesus.

So many times we think we have to say the right things. We feel the pressure of the moment pushing in on us as people unload a lifetime of confusion and hurt. Our job isn't to have the answer. Our job is to stay connected to Jesus so that we may at all times be a doorway to someone's destiny.

I love the way Martin Luther put it: "We are all mere beggars showing other beggars where the bread is." We are not bread makers. We are not bread salesmen. I think we would all walk a little taller and smile a little bigger if we realized this truth.

Have you ever been around someone who is just low maintenance? Like, they don't even have a suggestion for where they want to eat or what movie they want to see? They just travel light. Those are some of my favorite people to be around. They don't have all the answers and they are OK with admitting it. Not much frustrates them because they really just want other people to be happy. I am pretty sure Jesus was an expert at traveling light, and I believe that the life He is calling us to is so much simpler and satisfying than we could ever imagine.

In Matthew 11:28–30, Jesus dropped a profound truth bomb.

Come to me, all who labor and are heavy
laden, and I will give you rest. Take my
yoke upon you, and learn from me, for
I am gentle and lowly in heart, and you
will find rest for your souls. For my yoke
is easy, and my burden is light. -English
Standard Version

A *yoke* was a farming term and tool used around the necks of oxen as they were plowing fields. The yoke allowed a new ox that had never plowed a field to be yoked to a more seasoned ox that had been plowing fields for years. The young ox just followed the old wise ox each day and without even thinking about it would learn the pace and power of the old ox. God wants us to learn His pace and to walk in His power. That is why in this passage, He is saying, "Take my yoke upon you and learn from me." Walking with God is simply about walking with God. You didn't read that wrong; it's just that simple. Sometimes we complicate walking with God and make it about impossible standards and requirements. The less noticeable but equally important part of this scripture is that God has a field for each of us to plow. Each of us has an assignment and a purpose. It gives me so much excitement to remind you of this reality. God hasn't just dropped you into your current context and crossed His arms hoping you will figure out how to be effective. He placed you where He is already working and moving, and your only job is to walk with Him.

Sometimes we get so caught up watching other people's lives unfold that we are missing the joy of our own journeys with Jesus. My pastor, Judah Smith, recently said, "We are all following the same person but not the same path." God has a field for you to plow, and it looks different from my field. Some of us are trying to run onto other people's fields because we like theirs more than we like our own. But the grass isn't always greener. Both fields have the same contents but don't live in the same context. In other words, both fields will bear fruit, but they will have to weather different storms. God is in their fields for them and in your field for you. You and I will come alive and grow the most when we embrace our own paths and fields. I think many of us get tired of following Jesus because our lives don't resemble our friends' on Instagram and Facebook. Truthfully, we aren't tired of following Jesus—we are tired because we *aren't* following Jesus. Jesus says in this passage, "and you will find rest for your souls." This means that the outcome of following Jesus is rest, peace, and power—not comparison, self-deprecation, and pity.

Jesus doesn't desire that we find rest and reprieve from our work. He wants us to enjoy Him and allow that to redefine our work. Maybe even our desires. Could it be that we become most effective by letting go of fear and letting go of comfort? Is it possible that our real life is somewhere in the middle seat, waiting for us to look around and see the potential of the moment? Or maybe your real life is a haircut away?

I walked into my barbershop the other day trying to get that fade and then, BOOM—it happened. My barber began opening up about his whole life story with me. It started with abuse and ended with addiction. I sat in the chair and smirked without him seeing because just two hours earlier I felt the Lord telling me to pray for him. We talked for the next thirty minutes about everything you can possibly imagine. I asked him where he stood on God, and he quickly wanted to change the conversation to anything but God. I sensed years of disappointment behind the tone of his voice. I could relate to that unspoken feeling. I could see it in his body language. I was hurting with him and hurt even more knowing that God was the farthest thing from his mind. I just sat and listened and let him know that it was OK to vent. His pain didn't need an answer; his pain needed a listener. I got my fade and did my best to encourage his heart. I did my best to embrace the middle seat at my barbershop, and I will continue to do so. I want to keep being a place for him to drop some baggage in hopes that one day he picks up something much lighter.

The reality of this human experience is we all have baggage. We all struggle to let go of things that weigh us down. Those of us on our Christian journeys are not exempt from this. For the longest time, I was under the impression that following Jesus meant I could only talk about things that were light and easy. I could not allow my big baggage on the plane, but the irony is, that is exactly what Jesus wants us to do.

Can you imagine what your conversation would look like with Zebra Guy if he knew you brought a zebra on the plane, too? He wouldn't feel so judged anymore. He would feel like he made a true friend. A friend that cares and gets him. A friend that isn't out to point fingers or make him feel dumb for bringing the zebra. People will connect a lot better to your scars than your trophies. We have to be willing to feel the weight and struggle of someone else's baggage.

Maybe the baggage is self-doubt.

Maybe the baggage is depression.

Maybe the baggage is divorce.

Whatever it is, it's weighing them down. You know what that feels like right? To be weighed down by life's uncertainties and pain? Of course you do. Of course I do.

Prior to marrying my wife, I got cold feet. I was scared of marriage. I was scared of me trying to make marriage work. I saw two divorces fail before middle school and felt totally unprepared and inadequate to love another human being self-lessly. If my mother and father couldn't get it right, what made me think I could?

Cold feet were not even close to what I was feeling, to be honest. I was frozen. I had frostbite. I was frozen by fear and weighed down by baggage. My mom battled with depression for much of my childhood, and I remember thinking, "What if I become depressed?"

I felt like I was bringing so much baggage into our potential marriage, and that freaked me out. My potential wife, Jessica, was this strong and beautiful woman who needed a leader, not a boy who was afraid to fail. She needed a man who knew who he was and how to love.

Jessica came from an awesome, tight-knit family full of men and women who lived to make much of God and live in freedom. I was just a kid who had been uprooted a ton. A kid that had seen a lot of dysfunction and manipulation. If eHarmony or Christian Mingle were around during that time, they certainly would not have put us together as a match. I would have been in the Don't Even Look That Direction category! Seriously, if we all had to drag along our baggage, I would need a couple of semi-trucks and my wife might need a backpack.

I loved talking with Jessica when we first met. Even though her parents never got divorced, it was like she totally understood everything I was saying. Even though she grew up in one town her whole life, it was like she understood my story. The day I brought her all of my baggage and unloaded my heart in front of her was the day I thought we were done. Instead, Jessica taught me something that day. Life isn't about hiding our baggage—it's about opening and emptying it.

When we leave our baggage locked up on the inside, we may be insulating ourselves from hurt, but we are also isolating ourselves from healing. Jessica helped me heal . . . helped me come clean . . . helped me get real . . . helped me unpack twenty years of pain. As a counselor once told my father, "We all have unhealed hurts, unresolved issues, and unmet needs." That dude wasn't joking.

Jessica and I have been married for almost six years, and that journey still continues for both of us. We are committed to honesty and healing. We just had our first child! His name is Justice, and he is the greatest miracle of my life. He's an absolute stud.

I was so scared to have a kid. I was scared because I listened to the voices inside my head that told, "You don't know how to be a good dad." I heard this thought almost every day prior to having my son. I learned something valuable that I want to share with you.

The reality of our past has to bow down to the reality of God's Word. I am a son who has been adopted by God. I have had the perfect example of a father in Jesus. I have had the gentle love of a mother in Jesus. God has used every piece of my life to show how powerful He is. Where there was hurt and heartache in my family, God has infused restoration and life. It is an ongoing process, but I am confident that God won't stop until it's done.

I say all of this to point to God's willingness to use our baggage to make the world a better place. Your pain may be your greatest platform. Don't skim by that statement without considering the implications of it for your own life.

Growing up, I would do whatever I could to hide my story and hurt from people. Now I travel the nation pouring out old pain and offering real hope to students who are going through similar scenarios to what I went through as I kid. Many of them are experiencing far more difficult circumstances than I ever went through. This too has been a part of my healing process. Seeing the pain of others puts your own pain into perspective. It has a sobering effect.

My life as a youngster was filled with ups and downs, but it by no means was all bad. There were a ton of great moments. I had a stepfather who loved me, a mom who loved me, a sister who loved me, a stepmom who loved me, a stepbrother who loved me, a dad who loved me. Plus, I got a lot more Christmas gifts than most kids! Seriously, though, I am learning that God can do more with my baggage and honesty than I can do trying to act like they don't exist. Living an open life gives you the ability to heal. I have had conversations with complete strangers that have aided in my healing process, and that is a beautiful thing.

Noisy Love

Baggage causes us to live heavy, noisy, and disruptive lives. In 1 Corinthians 13:1 we see a pretty famous verse. It says, "If I speak in the tongues of men and of angels, but have not love, I am a noisy gong or a clanging cymbal" (English Standard Version). This is the verse that is most often heard at weddings. It sounds so poetic and Shakespearean. If you read this verse in your best Sean Connery, voice it's pretty awesome.

The cultural implications of this one verse are so powerful. It's referring to men and women of that time who used gongs and cymbals to worship false gods. Furthermore, they would do so in public theaters to draw attention to themselves. If you zoom out of the cultural implications and just look at the practical implications, you find a harsh but true reality: When our lives are void of love, we become disruptive like cymbals. Disruption causes separation but God's intention for love is to unify and connect.

As a drummer who got paid to bang on cymbals and make a ton of noise, I immediately look at this verse on a practical level. If I woke you up to the sound of one of my cymbals, you would be frustrated to say the least. When we are not experiencing and growing in our knowledge of God's love for us, we become self-centered. Our baggage (which we all have) begins to weigh us down instead of propelling us forward toward Christ. If you are following Jesus, just remember that you are following a person, not an idea or a concept.

Are you living a noisy disruptive life? Is your love caring or chaotic? These are hard but really good questions to ask. They are questions that when answered honestly can help us grow.

Is your time with Jesus rushed? If so, you will love people in a rushed sort of way. Walking with Jesus is not about hiding our baggage. Walking with people is not about hiding our baggage. Walking with Jesus is about *experiencing* a love you never thought possible, so that you can love others in a way you never thought possible.

What do you think might happen in your day today if you became a little more aware of God's love for you? How might that change the way you love others? What would that cause you to say? What would that help you to see?

When I live from my own strength or my own wisdom, I fail miserably at loving people. You and I will miss that mark every time. Dependency is more powerful than we could ever imagine. What we depend on is the most important part of the equation. People need to experience what we are leaning on. They need to see a love that is transforming us and captivating us from the inside out.

They need to see the baggage we have and are wrestling through. I know for some of us this may be a scary way to live life. But this type of vulnerability is like a romantic comedy; no matter how bad the storyline gets you and I both know it will end well. They all do!

Dependency causes people to be aware of whom we are dependent on: Jesus. We are not called to check our bags with Jesus. Jesus says, "Bring that hurt and anger on the plane." Jesus doesn't care that you haven't done your laundry in weeks. He's just glad you made the flight!

When you have an encounter with the unconditional love of Jesus, hiding is the last thing you want to do. Stuffing your bags in the dark and cold part of the plane is not His goal for you. He wants you to experience an exchange. You bring your whole heart, and in exchange, you get to walk with a whole new life—one that is filled with honesty. Transparency. Freedom. Some of us need to let Jesus back into the middle of our lives so we can learn how to love like He has loved us.

If you currently find yourself in a place of uncertainty in your journey with the Lord, just know that you are not alone. We have all gone through our fair share of tough times in our spiritual journeys. Don't keep reading and feeling like something is wrong with you. Nothing is wrong with you. You are normal, and you are OK. Take a moment to acknowledge God's desire to have and handle your baggage. If you are anything like me, you will need the following warning. Don't just give Him the fluffy and easy parts of your life. Give Him the heavy and yucky parts, too. Freedom comes when we lay it all down. Don't just live light in some areas of your life. That's still not freedom. Even light things will get heavy when you hold them for too long. Lay it all down.

CHAPTER 4: LANDING IN THE MIDDLE

I try to read a decent amount of books every year. I am always curious to know if people are writing from a place of knowledge or a place of experience. It's not at all that knowledge is bad, but personally, I want to be around people who have real-life experience—people who aren't regurgitating something they have heard, but rather are talking from a real-life perspective.

If books are written on paper, then experiences are written upon our hearts. I firmly believe that Jesus is calling us into an experience, an encounter, and an expedition. Not like a Ford Expedition; Jesus seems like the Prius type. No tinted windows.

He for sure would have a sunroof, though, so He could get better reception. Wait for it. Wait for it! For those of you who read for sport, you probably missed that joke. But let's be honest, it's a joke worth missing.

Anyway, just a couple of months ago while I was out of town, one of my wife's best childhood friends got into an accident while leaving her home here in Southern California. Abbie drives a car that is pretty low to the ground, so it is hard for her to see if cars are coming when pulling out of her apartment complex. Street parking in Cali makes the driving experience so enjoyable. (That sentence is drenched in sarcasm in case you were unsure.)

As Abbie inched her car forward, she quickly realized a car was approaching right toward her, and she had a split-second decision to make. She decided to hit the gas pedal and try to cross two lanes of traffic as quickly as possible in hopes of reaching the other side. The problem was, the girl coming toward her saw this happening and made the decision to change lanes at the exact same moment.

What resulted was a pretty horrific accident. To be honest, though, it wasn't an accident. Well, at least not to God. Abbie was OK but in a little bit of shock. Her body was pretty jostled by the brute force of the girl's car that smashed right into her driver's side door. Both cars were totaled. It appeared to be a pretty bad situation and one gigantic interruption for both of them.

To make matters worse, Abbie found out in this moment that the police don't even show up unless someone is intoxicated in the situation. I know. We are still scratching our heads about that one. From an outside perspective, this story is about as bad as it gets. You go from straightening your hair and brushing your teeth to BAM—a car accident within moments. Life is just crazy sometimes. There is no doubt about that.

But the best part of this story has yet to be told! Abbie and her new crash buddy began a conversation in the midst of the rubble. Through that conversation, Abbie realized that the girl had no family or friends to call while staring at her mangled car. Somewhere in the middle of the chaos Abbie saw an opportunity, a middle-seat moment. Abbie used the moment to learn a little bit about this perfect stranger. She didn't start quoting Scripture or leading the girl through some manufactured prayer. She saw an opportunity to befriend her. So Abbie invited her to the small group that my wife and I lead from our home every week. Guess who was the first person knocking at our door that week at 8 p.m.? If you're thinking it was the girl who collided with Abbie then your thinking is correct. Her name is Tennile. I figured it had to be someone new because nobody in our group is ever on time, including my wife and me (and the group meets in our home!). That car accident should have been one of the biggest obstacles of their year. Instead, it was the biggest opportunity of their year. Crazy, right?!

Here is the irony of all this. Abbie was on her way to go see a close friend of ours who was just admitted into the hospital and approved for a bone-marrow transplant. Abbie was already on a mission. She was already loving people. She was already doing something good with her day.

Maybe as you read this story you were thinking, "I already do _____." I think by and large we are all trying to do some good in our everyday lives. But what do you do when even your selfless schedule gets interrupted. When even your focus to help others gets royally thrown off and delayed?

What if we shifted our eyes from the mundane to the miracle? From the problem to the potential? It doesn't take super-spiritual Christians to be super effective. God wants to use every accident, incident, and interruption to show off His love to you and through you. I think many of us may feel like our faith is stale only because we aren't aware that God is in the small details and detours of life.

We have to remember that all we are and all we possess is His. I don't wish sickness or pain on anyone. But sometimes I see God move through sickness and pain in ways that are so amazing. I don't wish divorce or family tension on anyone, but I have seen God do some incredible things through both.

The verse that is ringing in my head right now is 2 Corinthians 12:9. "But he said to me, 'My grace is sufficient for you, for my power is made perfect in weakness.' Therefore I will boast all the more gladly of my weaknesses, so that the power of Christ may rest upon me,'" (English Standard Version).

It is not on us to be superheroes of the faith. It is not on us to perform for God. Some of us need to exhale and read that again. And by some of us, I mean me.

If you are anything like me, you have felt the pressures of life push in on you. I don't want to serve a God who needs me. I just don't deliver. I am just not that smart. I am not that loving or even reliable. I am not that perfect. I want to serve a God who wants me. A God who came to rescue and redeem me. A God who is so big and powerful that He can use someone who is so weak and needy.

When I look at the life of Jesus, I can't help but notice how good He is with bad people. He loves bad people. He loves broken people. His power is made perfect in our weakness. Not better. Not a little stronger. But perfect. Wow. Really, God? Perfect?

Me: "So what do I have to do, God?"

God: "Nothing. I will do the heavy lifting."

Me: "But, wait. I want to do something."

God: "OK. Enjoy my love, and love people out of that place."

Me: "OK. Yeah! That sounds great! Wait. How do I do that again?"

God: "Walk with me, son."

Me: "OK. I can do that! Wait. What does that look like, God?"

Walking with Jesus daily simply means believing that His way is better than ours. It is from this place that we see our deep need for God's daily presence. Walking with Jesus daily is about remembering what He has done for you. As we remember what God has done on our behalf, we begin every day with the realization that He alone is powerful. When He alone is our supreme power and authority, all of life gets put into proper perspective. We not only allow Him into every area of our lives, but we also excitedly hinge every decision on His guidance. God has something to say about sin and success. He has something to say about pain and prosperity. Walking with Jesus is about remembering, rehearsing, and enjoying the earthly and eternal benefits of His grace.

Whenever I am most confused about life, I come back to this simple reality. God wants my walk far more than He wants my work. It's not first about committing my work to God. This is about you and me being committed to walking with God every day.

So many of us get confused and give God our work, our dreams, and our schedules. We get frustrated when all these things don't go the way we want them to. We begin to wonder if God even cares about us in the least bit. If your idea of God's love is primarily connected to Him "coming through" on all of your desires then, friend—you will be gravely disappointed and confused in this life. He wants our hearts. He wants our desires far more than He wants our deeds. God wants us to lay it all down. To lay down the car accident right when it happens. To throw down the diagnosis at His feet. To give Him the permission to invade some of life's darkest and most confusing moments. Let's choose to invite Him to invade simple and seemingly insignificant detours.

When we invite Him, we need to know that He was actually already there waiting for us, preparing the moment, setting the stage, and controlling all the variables. Our invitation to Him really just activates our awareness of His constant presence and provision. Maybe the intimacy you really want with God is just as simple as letting go. So here is a question I ask myself a lot: What is distracting me right now? I challenge you to ask yourself this question and to lay whatever it is down so that you can live the life you were made to live.

Hope In Motion

My father-in-law, Joel, and I were sitting around one very hot summer night in Florida trying to come up with a name for our new nonprofit organization, a name that summed up the nature of the Gospel without sounding like an overtly Christian organization. It was getting late and the only word coming to mind was *hope*. We were restless because we felt like the Gospel isn't just hope; it moves, as well. It moves toward the broken and hurting. So naturally the word *motion* poured out of his mouth, and then we had it: Hope In Motion!

Hope In Motion exists to share a message of hope with students in public schools across the world. We invite those students who experience our motivational school presentation into settings where we can boldly proclaim the love of Jesus through music, a message, and a time for response. Our organization is focused on three simple but very clearly defined things:

1. Demonstration

2. Proclamation

3. Transformation

I want to take some time to talk about these three different areas that I believe are so powerful and essential to Gospel-centered living.

Demonstration is the most essential part of our faith. It is all about what our lives are saying and very little about what our mouths are saying. I believe that people are looking toward the Church not to hear an eloquent message, but to see a group of people who have genuine love for one another and for humanity. The book of John points to this with such beautiful clarity. John 13:35 "'By this all people will know that you are my disciples, if you have love for one another,'" (English Standard Version).

How do we learn how to love people? The answer is simple: Spend time being loved on by God. We can't serve God without hearing from God. Jesus is our greatest example of demonstrative love. Every step of the way, we see Him demonstrating the compassion, authority, and mercy of God. Demonstration has nothing to do with performance and everything to do with a deep love for people in every moment of our lives. We get this from spending time with Jesus.

What would your office place look like if you were living with this mindset every single day? What would your school campus look like? I will tell you what it would like: Hope In Motion!

That is the nature of the Gospel. It is not stagnant. It is not archaic and boring. It's alive. It's ready. It's willing. It's for the here and the now! The Gospel is on its toes, anxiously awaiting all those who want it.

Proclamation is often what we are best at as a Church. We love to proclaim how much we know about Jesus. But what if the world is not so interested in how much we know about Jesus? What if they are looking for an encounter with Him? When we speak about Jesus, it's important that it is coming from a real place. That probably sounds vague, so let me try again. It is vital that we know what we believe about Christ so we can clearly articulate and not complicate the Gospel. It's great that we can sit for hours and talk about predestination and whether we are five-point Calvinists, but at some point in our own personal faith we have to be able to answer this one question: Who is Jesus? Our understanding of Jesus has to be rooted in the Word of God and not our opinions, feelings, or ideals. When the world hears one Church proclaiming one Jesus, we will see true hope in motion.

We experience God through His word.

Through His church.

By walking with Him every day.

Through learning to love like He loves. To see like He sees.

Proclaiming is not about knowledge. It is about rehearsing God's love for us every day and talking about it whenever He tells us to.

If you and I can tell where people are from by their accents, then people should be able to tell you follow Jesus by your accent. We should speak more and more like He speaks.

We should be a people looking to build with our words and not burn. When we encounter someone looking to gossip, we should cover the moment with grace and gentleness. Plainly put, this is what it truly means to proclaim Jesus. We speak like Him, serve like Him, love like Him.

Transformation is my favorite part of the Gospel. This is what the Word of God promises and assures us—transformation! The good news of the Gospel is that everything changes when Jesus enters our hearts. You can't hear the word *transformation* and not think of the movie *Transformers*. All of the Transformers in their disguised states are pretty simple and ordinary looking. But when the moment calls for it, they are able to transform into these massive and powerful pieces of machinery. It is in this state that they are able to take on evil and protect humanity.

Isn't that a beautiful description of what we are supposed to be as the Church? When we live lives that have been and are continually being transformed by the Gospel, we are living in our most powerful state. It is here that we are able through the power and authority of God's word to take on evil and share the hope of Jesus. Transformation is hope in motion. It is H.I.M. See what just happened? If not, it's OK. I am a little slow to pick up on little clues myself. Transformation moves us to loving like Jesus. As we spend time imitating God, we learn how to activate God-like love. We activate a love that moves beyond affection and into self-sacrificing service to others. Ephesians speaks on this so clearly.

Ephesians 5:1–2 from The Message says:

> Watch what God does, and then you do it, like children who learn proper behavior from their parents. Mostly what God does is love you. Keep company with him and learn a life of love. Observe how Christ loved us. His love was not cautious but extravagant. He didn't love in order to get something from us but to give everything of himself to us. Love like that.

Community

Some months back, I began a pretty challenging journey out of the comfort of the music industry into full-time ministry. Playing drums for Christian artists has enabled me to learn and grow so much. I am so grateful to artists like KJ-52, Group 1 Crew, Anthem Lights, Rhema Soul, and so many more who have encouraged me and challenged me all the same. I got a taste of community while traveling the nation. I got a taste of what it means to not just be in proximity, but to also be in a personal relationship with humans who are chasing after the heart of God.

I can't even begin thinking about writing a book like this and not saying thank you to these world changers. You all truly changed my world for the better. Thank you.

I have stories that have been imprinted on my mind and heart during the last eight years, so many that I could probably just write a book of road stories. All the stories are very different. All have different nuances, but they all have one thing in common. All of them point to a loving God.

I have seen some of these artists get taken advantage of financially, cheated out of stage time, or treated like second-rate citizens. All of these men and women have exemplified love in those moments. Even in their disappointment and frustration, they have managed to speak well of others.

I have seen many choose people over business pressures time and time again. I can recall instances where friends worked diligently on a plane trying to finish writing songs, yet they willingly paused to encounter the needs of the person sitting next to them. I have seen friends stay up late in hotel lobbies and council leaders that need them because they are in some really tough situations.

Why? Are they just "Super Christians"? Of course not. They are humans with real schedules, real deadlines, and real families who all require their time and attention. They have real responsibilities pressing in on them, just like you and I do. But what is even more real in them is their abilities to tune in to

Christ. They have a real knowledge and understanding of God's voice and an awareness for what He is doing around them in their everyday lives.

When you follow Jesus, you begin feeling your priorities being reprioritized by God. He does this because He wants His children to live full and effective lives, lives that are marked by a love that is not from planet Earth. A love that cannot be manufactured or even maintained by anything other than the very presence of God himself dwelling in and through us. In the book of Romans, I believe Paul points us to how this type of love is possible.

Romans 8:14–16 says:

> For all who are led by the Spirit of God are children of God. So you have not received a spirit that makes you fearful slaves. Instead, you received God's Spirit when he adopted you as his own children. Now we call him, "Abba, Father." For his Spirit

joins with our spirit to affirm that we are

God's children. -New Living Translation

We are children of God. We have been adopted. I don't know if you have ever met people who were adopted. Even though they does not have the same DNA as their parents, it's at times very difficult to know that. Their countenance and mannerisms all point to them being family. Even their vocal tones and quirky habits can be just like their parents'. It's actually really cool. In the same way their parents have adopted them into their family they have adopted their family into their hearts. They don't see themselves as outsiders who don't belong. They know they are loved because their parents actually chose them. Like, sought them out. They saved hard-earned money and got in a car or on a plane and loved them so directly and intentionally.

Humanity became God's highest priority. God's love moves toward us in the same manner. God's love in us also moves toward others in the same manner. God's love is moving toward your co-workers. God's love is moving toward your next-door neighbor and even your childhood friend who is as lost as that one sock in your dryer.

God is ready to invade our schedules and our checklists. As we spend time with God our preferences and priorities begin to change. It yet again all begins with an awareness of God's love. God has adopted me, and He went above and beyond in the payment for my soul. I have not only been adopted from my old life, but I have been adopted into a new life, a new community.

I think many us have pretty skewed perceptions of community. This is so much more than the people who live in proximity to us. Community is the essence of the Gospel. The Father, the Son, and the Holy Spirit. They serve different parts but they are no less unified and communing with one another.

What is *community*? Google defines *community* as: "A group of people living in the same place or having a particular characteristic in common. A feeling of fellowship with others, as a result of sharing common attitudes, interests, and goals."

Well, if we use that definition as a spring board toward further exploring community than we must conclude that community is a place of belonging. Businesses all over the world have developed infrastructure that is centered on creating a feeling of community, a feeling of belonging. Maybe there is something here for us to see.

McDonald's has done an exceptional job of creating community. Chick-fil-A has done the same and probably even a better job at it. These are businesses that have made it their business to create community. To make people feel welcomed and valued. To play music that creates a sense of peace. To have a place for kids to play and meet other kids. To always say, "My pleasure." We look forward to these familiar two words from employees at Chick-fil-A because they make us feel loved, valued, and dare I say, at home.

Why? Because when you know you belong, you begin to believe that this is home.

When you and I feel accepted, our walls come down and our true selves come out. Belonging precedes belief. We have an opportunity in every middle-seat moment with people to bring a sense of true community. We do this in many ways but ultimately by finding and creating common ground.

Some of my deepest conversations with people have started with, "Dude, that watch is so dope." I know, super spiritual, right? Other conversations have started with, "Where are you headed?" The point is, when we are being led by the Spirit we find ourselves being community creators.

We should be known for our inclusiveness.

We should be known for our invitations.

We should be known for being listeners and lovers.

We should be known for our ridiculous generosity.

These are all things that will naturally grow in us as we allow God's Word to take root in us.

It's actually a little weird when it starts happening! I remember recent times when I had small amounts of money in the bank but picked up the tab with a few people at the table like I was a millionaire. Then I was like, "Shoot, what am I thinking?"

But God always meets our needs. We are never lacking or without. If anything, we always end up with leftovers, with plenty to pass around. He is faithful in every sense of the word. Don't be scared to leverage your life for the good of people; it actually may be the very mark that you are walking with Jesus.

Community has been what has made this recent life transition for me possible. My wife and I lead community groups for our church here in Southern California and we love it! What could be more awesome than creating a space where people feel at home?

Our pastor, Judah Smith, and his family fly in from Seattle Washington to share the Gospel with a community that is growing rapidly in Beverly Hills. We are all watching God do amazing things in a culture that is inundated with moral corruption and greed. As you probably know, that is not limited to Los Angeles or Beverly Hills. It's a human issue. More than a thousand people are gathering each week and meeting in hotels, and we are all leaning into God's heart for us. His design for us. His community.

Every week a group of about twenty-five people come to our home to hang with my wife and me. We talk about life. We talk about gigs that fell through. We talk about our families that we miss across the country. We talk about sin that we are struggling to get past. We talk about God's crazy love for us. It never gets old. All of this is aided by good food and coffee, of course.

What's most interesting about our group is that new people continue to show up! Have you ever been a part of something so good that you just have to tell everyone about it? That's what happens in our group and what's happening across our church. People are inviting friends that are in their everyday lives to hang, belong, and come home. Our aim isn't that people be converted to a certain faith but that they leave knowing God loves them and there are some people who love them, as well.

These twenty-five people and counting have challenged me in so many ways. My home often doesn't feel full unless they are in it. I love the noise, the people venting about their weeks. The people walking in with frustration about the Los Angeles traffic. That struggle is real, you guys. Real horrible!

All of us come in with the weight of the week on our shoulders, including me. We don't always leave with answers. But we leave knowing that we are not alone. We leave knowing that we belong and that God loves us all so deeply.

What if I told you that you could create this type of community in just a few moments with perfect strangers? Just a few moments of conversation can let people know "I am not alone." I truly believe community is what will cause change in our lives through communing with God and communing with people. It is here that love will speak louder than doctrine. It is here that my true theology about God has been shaken and reinforced. It is here that I have learned to love and honestly be loved in return.

I got into a car accident the other day. It was just a little fender bender and even though the lady slammed on her breaks for no good reason I was still at fault because I hit the back of her car. Still baffled by how that works! As she got out of the car she was talking to someone in the backseat and saying, "Are you OK, baby?" I quickly saw that her little girl was in a car seat. As a new father, I immediately began to exude concern for the little girl and her mom. I started apologizing even though moments before I didn't want to. But it was my fault, so I did. We exchanged information, and I did everything I could to let her know that it was my bad. To be honest with you right now, I was going to a coffee shop to vent to a friend. My father was recently given a little more than a year to live, and I couldn't see straight ever since I got the news. I wasn't in the best place to be thinking about creating community or loving people the way God loves me. I didn't realize it but just my "I'm sorry" did something for this woman.

I got a text from her the next day that yet again taught me the power of middle-seat moments. It said this:

I JUST WANTED YOU TO LET YOU KNOW THAT YOUR INSURANCE COMPANY HAS BEEN REALLY GOOD TO ME AND THEY

ARE TAKING CARE OF ALL THE THINGS THAT NEEDED TO BE FIXED.

Later she texted:

I DIDN'T KNOW THAT YOU ARE A MOTIVATIONAL SPEAKER FOR CHILDREN/YOUTH. I SAW SOME OF YOUR YOUTUBE VIDEOS. YOU AND YOUR WIFE ARE VERY INSPIRING. I JUST HAVE TO SAY THAT ON THE DAY OF THE ACCIDENT WAS MY GRANDPA'S DEATH ANNIVERSARY AND I TOTALLY FORGOT ABOUT IT. I AM NOT SURE IF YOU BELIEVE IN **FATE** BUT I THINK IT'S MY GRANDPA TAPPING ME AND REMINDING ME TO LOOK UP AND SAY HI AND REMINDING ME HOW LUCKY I AM TO HAVE A BEAUTIFUL LIFE WITH MY CHILDREN. THANK YOU!"

My response to her:

GOSH . . . I'M SO HUMBLED BY YOUR WORDS! STILL FEEL TERRIBLE THAT I COULDN'T STOP FAST ENOUGH!! I TOTALLY GET WHAT LOSS FEELS LIKE. I'M IN THE PROCESS OF LOSING MY FATHER TO BONE CANER AS WE SPEAK. THE PAIN IS REAL. I WAS ACTUALLY ON MY WAY TO MEET WITH A FRIEND FOR COFFEE TO VENT A LITTLE AND PROCESS MY PAIN OUT LOUD. WELL IF FOR NOTHING ELSE MAYBE GOD ALLOWED THIS TO HAPPEN TO LET YOU KNOW THAT YOU'RE NOT ALONE IN YOUR PAIN! I'M SO GLAD THAT THE INSURANCE IS HANDLING THINGS SWIFTLY. PRAYING FOR YOUR CONTINUED SAFETY AND JOURNEY THROUGH THIS LIFE!

Her response to me:

I'M SO SORRY ABOUT YOUR FATHER, I WILL BE PRAYING FOR YOU AND YOUR FAMILY. PLEASE DON'T FEEL BAD ABOUT THE ACCIDENT, I'M JUST GLAD THAT WE ARE NOT SERIOUSLY HURT. HAVE A BLESSED DAY!!

My response to her:

YOU AS WELL! GOD BLESS.

People are watching us. I very easily could have gotten out of that car screaming and yelling. I wasn't emotionally stable in that moment by any stretch of the imagination. But my apology opened some sort of door in her. Maybe this whole community thing isn't so hard. Maybe for you, community will begin with an "I'm so sorry."

Out of all the millions of people I could have bumped into that day, I bumped into the one who could relate to what

I was feeling in that moment. She reminded me that I wasn't alone. She showed me that community can start even through a fender bender. I am positive that you will have hundreds of middle-seat moments just in the next few days of your life. Some types of community are forged over years, and other types are formed in a moment.

What if you stopped waiting for them?

What if you started looking for them and anticipating them?

What if you started creating them?

So many stories are waiting to be told and so many lives are waiting to be touched.

CHAPTER 5: FREE TO ROAM

We live in a time full of tension. Racial tension. Economic tension. Global tension. Everywhere we turn there is hurt, heartache, and habits that have been nagging all of us daily. The problem seems so big and so deeply rooted. I think we are all wondering how this will get fixed.

I know you know this, but it's all a sin issue. All the hurt and brokenness can be traced back to the garden. So it's not just that we are living in broken times, but it is also that we are a broken people. For those of you who have trusted Jesus with your entire being, you are being made new. You are the agent for change on Earth until Jesus comes back and makes all things right. We should be the breath of fresh air.

Choosing to focus in on God's ability and not our own is where we find meaning and fulfillment. The infamous tax collector Zack (AKA Zacchaeus) did not climb a tree to be seen, but rather to see Jesus. He wanted to learn grace from the source of all grace. Jesus went on to invite himself over for a sleepover with Zack. I think Jesus wanted him to know that grace had to invade his most vulnerable place. His home. His heart. The place he lets down his guard and isn't known for his successes or failures. Truthfully, I believe that lasting change happens when we allow Jesus into our hearts. Maybe you are reading this and trying to get a perspective about who Jesus is. Just like my boy Zack, you are climbing some sort of tree to try to gain a new perspective on life and all its meaning. In my own life, I have climbed many trees all to realize the only tree that will give me the right perspective is that of the Cross. All other trees may give you a perspective but not the perspective that will change your whole existence.

What trees exist in your life right now?

Where do you run on a daily basis to find perspective, hope, and meaning? Whatever tree you may be climbing right now, I want you to know that if you're looking for satisfaction, look to the Cross. Zack had an encounter with Jesus in his home that changed his life forever. Just like Zack, we need encounters with Jesus in our hearts. This type of encounter will afford you and I an ability to be loved and then in return love others, no matter how great the offense.

Recently, as you may remember, there was a terrible shooting in Charleston, South Carolina. A twenty-one-year-old young man walked into a prayer meeting at a local church and shot nine people. He killed nine people who were calmly seeking God's guidance and love.

As I write this portion of the book I am sitting in a coffee shop in southern California, and I am looking at a picture of the shooter on my soon-to-time-out Wi-Fi connection. I am considering the reality of how powerful love is. I have my headphones off, and I can hear a couple of conversations happening all around me.

One young guy is asking another young lady for advice on how to break into the film business. Two girls at a separate table are in a deep conversation about relational issues in their family. A young girl sitting behind me is drawing an unbelievable portrait of someone in her notebook. Another guy is sitting by himself just watching all the people walk in and out. He looks lonely. This may seem a little dark, but track with me for second.

What if there was a shooter in this room right now? I am not even talking about someone with a gun. I am talking about a person who is ready to give up on a dream and shoot down years of hard work and investment. What if there is someone in here who is ready to give up on his or her marriage? What if there is someone in here who is so sick of the monotony of life that they are ready to give up entirely? In a room this size, there is a ton of hurt and a ton of uncertainty.

What if I zoomed out and considered the implications of God having me here today writing these words? I am not Jesus, obviously. But if it's true that His presence is living and active inside of me, I have to be willing to consider His desire for moments like this one. What if you were the person who could change the future with how you love right now? Love is the only force that can affect the past, the present, and the future. The more we breathe in God's love for us the more we exhale God's love for people. There is power in this reality. Jesus lived in this reality. Jesus wants us to live in this reality.

Friends, the problem of brokenness in this world is real. But the problem is bigger than prejudice or religious practice. What we are seeing is a symptom to a much bigger problem. You and I know all to well what the problem is: sin. But do we have an awareness that Jesus living in us and through us is the answer? I don't like living in the past. I actually have a saying that I try to live by. It goes: "I will only look back if it helps me look forward." I don't want to spend my life looking through the smallest mirror in the proverbial car, the rearview. I want to embrace what's in front of me and enjoy the moment. But in this case, I want us to consider the "what if" to this shooting.

What if this young man would have had a middle-seat moment with a believer? What if he would have been loved and listened to long enough to help him become aware of a loving and personal God. A God who sent His son to deal with the racial angst that was in his heart. A God who wants to redefine his skewed, false reality of people and give him a clear picture of unity and love.

This isn't me living in the past. This is me simply saying that we have to see the importance of where we have been placed right here in this moment. God wants to activate the reality of love in and through us. Every moment matters when love is a part of every moment.

Pass the Salt Please

In Matthew 5:13–16, we are identified in scripture as "salt and light" (English Standard Version). God doesn't just call us to be salt and light, but He also *identifies* us as salt and light. In other words, He doesn't say, "You are becoming this." He says, "You *are* this. This is why you are here."

We should be the light in the darkness.

We should be the salt of the earth.

Providing flavor.

Providing healing and hope.

Providing preservation and covering.

But how? How do we go about doing this?

I have asked that question for the majority of my life. The answer can't be found in what we are doing. It is a state of being. Maybe you have heard it said, "We are not human doings, we are human beings." It's true. We all know that salt adds flavor. Some of you put salt on your food before you even taste the food to figure out if it needs it. But is that it? Are we just here to add flavor? I mean, I'm cool with adding a little flavor everywhere I go. That sounds pretty fun, actually. I think Jesus wants believers to be the life of the party. I don't mean just the center of attention. Everyone has met that guy before at the party! Instead, He wants us to add value and peace so that people let down their guards and open their hearts.

But what else does salt do? Salt preserves. Salting food such as meat and fish before it's cooked is one of the oldest methods for preserving food. We are called to be preservation. To keep things alive. To keep people alive. To encourage people's dreams and destinies. To bring life in the midst of death. Preservation is also a way of keeping food from decay, from growing fungus or bacteria. This means that we can help people to not grow bitter on the inside. We can help friends war against the decaying effects of anger, fear, and racial strife.

What an intense picture of what God is using us to be in this world! We add flavor. We preserve life! As if those two things aren't enough, we see one more powerful characteristic of salt. It heals wounds.

When I was a kid I used to love going to the beach but I hated swimming in the ocean. The idea of not being able to see what was around me freaked me out. Call me faithless if you want, but I call it common sense. If you can't see your toes through the water, don't get in. I was in middle school when my mom told me that the ocean water would be good for my acne. When you are in middle school, how you look is pretty much the most important part of your life.

So once I figured this out, I quickly got over my fear of the water and went out far enough to immerse myself in the salty awesomeness! That salt water would clear my acne within a couple of days each time we went to the beach! It was crazy. And that's how I got a date to the middle-school dance! Just kidding. But wouldn't that be funny? I can picture middle-school kids across the globe jetting for the waters.

We have the privilege as Jesus followers of being an open source of healing that all of humanity can immerse in. We are here to put our hands to the wounds. Sometimes the wounds are deep and ugly. Sometimes they are surface level and relatively simple.

Either way one thing is certain: There is a lot of hurt in the world around us. This means there is a lot of opportunity for salt to come in handy. Being salt is not about having the answers. It's about offering flavor where it is needed. Preservation where it is needed. Healing where and when it is needed. That is who we are, so stay salty, my friends.

Salt will turn on the lights in this dark world. It will illuminate a new Kingdom that is coming and, dare I say, the Kingdom that is already here. Salt is the stuff of God's Kingdom; so therefore, we are the stuff of God's Kingdom. When we live salty lives, we are bringing God's Kingdom to Earth! That's worth another exclamation point!

Taxiing to the Gate

If you have never trusted Jesus as your personal Savior, I want to point you toward Scripture. This is not for the sake of religion, but for the sake of your own soul being awakened to the truth about God. He is not angry with you. He is not waiting for some formal apology.

This could be a middle-seat moment for your soul. Right here. Right now.

Please take a moment to escape from the ankle-deep opinions of man and popular culture.

The book of John captures these powerful words in John 3:16–17:

> For God loved the world so much that he gave his one and only Son, so that every-one who believes in him will not perish but have eternal life. God sent his Son into the world not to judge the world, but to save the world through him. -New Living Translation

God's love is reaching in our direction. The Bible says, "If you confess with your mouth that Jesus is Lord and believe in your heart that God raised him from the dead, you will be saved" (Romans 10:9, English Standard Version). Your confession is linked to your awareness of you not being God. If you and I confess that we are not God, then we are opening the door for Jesus to come in and make our hearts His home.

If you made that confession and have asked Jesus to be your Lord, I want to stress a few very crucial thoughts to you.

Number 1: Congratulations! You will spend eternity knowing, seeing, and experiencing God.

Number 2: God wants you to start enjoying Him now. He wants to talk to you and comfort you.

Number 3: It's imperative that you find a local church that can help you grow and live like Jesus.

Number 4: It's not going to be easy! You are choosing His nature, His power, and His truth over your own.

Number 5: With Jesus, anything is possible. Your past is covered in Him. Your present is sustained by Him. Your future is known by Him. Exhale.

Bonus: Jesus is the only perfect one you can count on. The church will let you down at times but that's why the church isn't built on the people but on the person and work of Jesus. Don't forfeit the power of community because of minor disagreements or personality types. Cover people in love and enjoy the many benefits of knowing, being known, and making Him known.

Your life matters, and here is how you can make it count. Paul's words to the Roman church seem fitting right here:

Romans 12:1–2 of The Message says:

Place Your Life Before God

> So here's what I want you to do, God helping you: Take your everyday, ordinary life—your sleeping, eating, going-to-work, and walking-around life—and place it before God as an offering. Embracing what God does for you is the best thing you can do for him. Don't

become so well-adjusted to your culture that you fit into it without even thinking. Instead, fix your attention on God. You'll be changed from the inside out. Readily recognize what he wants from you, and quickly respond to it. Unlike the culture around you, always dragging you down to its level of immaturity, God brings the best out of you, develops well-formed maturity in you.

This is what we were made to do!

We were made to be focused and concerned with the lives of others. We have to see that the rhythm of our lives should mirror that of Jesus. The world is wondering what to do and where to turn. We live in a time where questions are far more common than answers.

People need *the* answer. My prayer is that they look no further than the middle seat.

Jesus at the Center

Jesus always found himself in the center of real-life situations. I have always been so blown away by His ability to insert himself into life's most frustrating and painful moments. If it wasn't the woman at the well, then it was a group of Pharisees in the synagogue. Jesus handled each situation a little differently. I really believe that this speaks volumes to how He wants us to be in the midst of this life. He wants us to remain sensitive to the fact that we can't just have cliché answers to life's toughest problems.

Sometimes He would proclaim truth and cause men to drop the stones in their hands. Sometimes He would call out someone's struggle and offer him or her something greater. On other occasions, we see Jesus not saying a word, almost as if He wants us to know that His very presence is enough.

Despite how we view His actions we can certainly draw this one conclusion about His life: He loved getting into the center of situations, circumstances, and moments. He knew that by positioning himself in the center of all the stories, people would eventually get it.

"I am the way, the truth, and the life. No one comes to the Father except through me" (John 14:6, English Standard Version). Jesus is the invitation to the greatest family party of all time—eternity! From beginning to end, it's always been about Jesus. The entire biblical narrative points to Jesus. He is the center of everything. He longs to be at the center of your everything. He literally stepped out of eternity to give humanity an opportunity to engage and enjoy Him. The middle-seat lifestyle is embodied in the person and work of Jesus Christ. It's all about us realizing that God has strategically placed each of us right where we are in this very moment.

Whether you are in your college dorm room or you're on the metro heading into the city. Whether you are in a coffee shop looking out to the sunset, or you are about to go sit in a cubical. God is with you. God is for you.

If you have trusted Jesus as your personal Savior, then He has made your soul His dwelling place. God wants our lives to demonstrate and proclaim the transformative power of the Gospel. You and I get to be the invitation for someone to enjoy and experience the saving power of Jesus! How awesome is that?

Every moment of your life places you into the center of someone else's story. That someone else could be ready to give up. That someone else may be burnt out on religion. That someone else may be near death because of a disease. At the end of the day, *that* someone needs you to portray *the* someone: Jesus.

We all know the story of Jesus, but there is one thing we overlook at times. The crucifixion was Jesus' last moments on planet Earth as a man. He was dying on that Cross for the sins of the world as a sacrifice for all mankind. Isn't that enough? Hasn't He done enough for all of us already?

Sometimes we overlook the most beautiful moments in His story. Jesus is hanging on that Cross feeling the wrath of God to its utmost degree, both spiritually and physically. It was no accident that even in that moment He was strategically positioned between two men. More specifically, He was between two criminals who deserved the punishments they were getting.

Go there with me for a second. One man on His left. One man on His right. One man a skeptic and one man a confessed sinner. Notice who was in the middle seat: Jesus. King of all kings and ruler of all things. He lived a sinless life and was now dying a criminal's death.

Even in this gruesome moment where He could have been thinking, "I have done enough, my mission is complete," He still chose to extend grace. Although Jesus spent His last moments in pain, He didn't allow His momentary agony to keep Him from seeing the eternal opportunity. Jesus could barely breathe, but He chose to use His pain as a platform. This short but powerful conversation had eternal implications for the criminal.

In the same way, I believe it is possible that the brief conversation with the person next to you has eternal implications. In the midst of His suffering, the heart of Jesus was focused on others.Only love can move beyond that kind of pain. Only love will help us see the opportunities all around us.

STOP.

When was the last time you truly paused and inhaled God's love toward you? Don't rush past this truth. It is fundamental. Foundational. Imperative. At the onset of this book I exposed a daunting thought that actually crossed my mind. The thought was, "Have you ever not gotten something you deserved?" Although I have had thought this to myself countless times, there was something so much more myopic and gross about this particular time.

The reality is that my life is now centered around this very thought. "It should have been me . . . on that Cross." But thank God that in His goodness I didn't get what I deserved. Mercy was shown toward me so that I didn't get the condemnation I deserved. Instead, grace gave me what I didn't deserve: Freedom. Joy. Peace. Perspective.

Maybe this is why Scripture points us toward renewing our minds daily. Daily, we set our sights on the person of Jesus. We zoom in to observe His kind of love. In the person of Jesus, we get a front row seat into what it means to live the middle-seat life. We see the heart and nature of our Jesus. It's one of love, compassion, and deep grace for criminals.

Criminals like me.

Criminals like you.

This is where we deplane and part ways. Whether you're on a layover, headed home, or going to the opposite end of the Earth, may Christ remain your model. As you go about your everyday life, choose people. Every time, over and over again, choose people!

I want the last words of this book to be for my new son, Justice.

Son, Daddy loves you! I don't care how old or big you get, I never want to stop telling you that I love you.

I have been on stages in front of thousands.

I have sat next to influential people from around the world.

I have dreamed and journeyed far and wide.

Nothing compares to the love I have for you and your Mama. Home is by far my greatest adventure.